PUB WA

— I N —

South Wales

THIRTY CIRCULAR WALKS
AROUND SOUTH WALES INNS

Paul Traynor

COUNTRYSIDE BOOKS
NEWBURY, BERKSHIRE

COUNTRYSIDE BOOKS
3 Catherine Road
Newbury, Berkshire

ISBN 1 85306 313 4

Publisher's Note

We hope that you obtain considerable enjoyment from this book; great care has been taken in its preparation. However, changes of landlord and actual closures are sadly not uncommon. Likewise, although at the time of publication all routes followed public rights of way or well-established permitted paths, diversion orders can be made and permissions withdrawn.

We cannot accept responsibility for any inaccuracies, but we are anxious that all details covering both pubs and walks are kept up to date, and would therefore welcome information from readers which would be relevant to future editions.

Designed by Mon Mohan
Cover illustration by Colin Doggett
Photographs and maps by the author

Produced through MRM Associates Ltd., Reading
Typeset by Paragon Typesetters, Queensferry, Clwyd
Printed and bound in England by J. W. Arrowsmith Ltd., Bristol

Contents

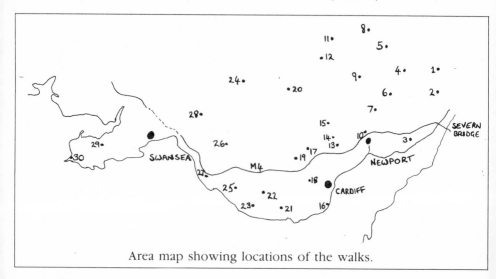

Area map showing locations of the walks.

Introduction

It is a tourism cliché to claim to be a 'region of contrasts' but South Wales can truly justify that sales pitch. To the east lies the Wye Valley – a scenic gem admired for centuries. To the west is the Gower Peninsula, with its superb beaches and cliffs. In between you have the rolling farmland and attractive villages of the Vale of Glamorgan; the Heritage Coast of the Welsh underbelly; miles of unspoilt rural charm in eastern Gwent; and, of course, the famous Valleys – once the industrial powerhouse of Britain.

The Brecon Beacons and the Black Mountains are perhaps the best-known areas in southern Wales for 'serious' walking. These upland areas are well covered by many guides and I make no apology for largely steering clear of them. This is a book of pub walks, mostly of modest length, which anyone in reasonably good shape can enjoy.

To practical matters. While the route directions should guide you safely around each walk, the sketch maps are intended only as a rough guide and should be used with the relevant Ordnance Survey map. No special navigational skills should be required in good weather, but caution should come first if mist falls or if visibility is poor. Do not hesitate to turn back if you become unsure about where to go.

The usual advice applies concerning clothing and footwear. Welsh weather is notoriously fickle. Even in high summer it is best to take spare warm clothing and a waterproof jacket – winds can be chilly. It seems a rule of walking that however dry underfoot the bulk of a given route may be, there will be one gloriously soggy bit. Good boots are a worthwhile investment for longer walks and gaiters are often useful. On shorter walks, wellies may be best after wet weather.

Pub opening hours are not specified because they are frequently changed these days. Some pubs open longer in summer and at weekends, for example. If you are likely to turn up expecting to eat outside normal hours (12 noon to 2 pm; 7 pm to 9 pm), it is best to call in advance to check.

Most pubs are happy for their car parks to be used as bases – provided you intend to give them your custom later. It is always a good idea, where possible, to mention what you are doing. A polite enquiry about where children are welcome and whether muddy boots are acceptable is diplomatic.

Whether you pub first and walk later, or vice versa, may I wish you many hours of happy hiking and relaxed refreshment.

Paul Traynor
spring 1994

1 Penallt
The Boat Inn

A row of muddy boots in the porch is confirmation of one reason for this cosy pub's popularity. On the Welsh bank of the Wye, it is a handy refuelling point for two long distance paths: the Offa's Dyke Path and the Wye Valley Walk. The pub stands almost alone, opposite the English village of Redbrook, to which it is connected by footbridge. More than 350 years old, it originally served the boat trade plying up and down the Wye. Walkers and canoeists enjoying the exercise and superb scenery now provide passing custom of a different sort.

The healthy, wholesome food and good beers are just the ticket in this area of outdoor activity. Everything is home cooked and the pub reverses the great British tradition of 'chips with everything' – chips are not served! All meals come with salads and jacket potatoes and are very reasonably priced. Options range from locally smoked salmon to filled jacket potatoes or turkey and mushroom crumble. Vegetarians will appreciate the good selection, with pan haggerty (cheese, onion, potato and garlic pie) a particularly popular choice. Real ale fans face a hard bout of decision making as there is usually a range of eight or nine beers, for example, Theakston Old Peculier, Courage Directors and Wadworth 6X.

Telephone: 0600 712615.

How to get there: It is easiest to park in Redbrook and walk across the footbridge. Go south from Monmouth across the Wye on the A466. After about 3 miles reach the Redbrook Rovers football club car park on the right – the pub shares the car park. The footbridge is adjacent. (NB there is no right turn from the A40 heading north – go past the bridge, and turn around at the next roundabout.)

Parking: There is limited car parking near the pub. The car park in Redbrook offers more space.

Length of the walk: About 3 ½ miles. Map: OS Landranger series 162 Gloucester and Forest of Dean area (GR 536098).

This hilly circuit, less challenging than some of the circular routes based on the Offa's Dyke Path or Wye Valley Walk, stays on the Welsh side of the Wye, exploring an attractive tangle of lanes and paths in an area renowned for its scenic beauty.

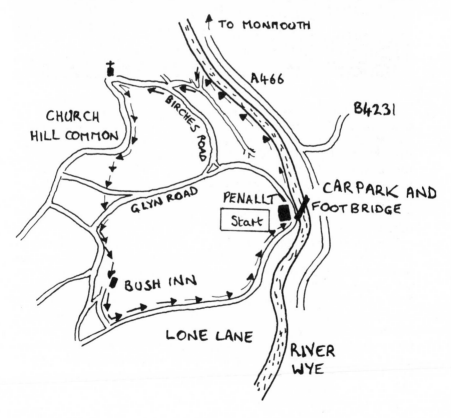

The Walk

With your back to the pub, turn left and go through the bridlegate on the river bank. Continue on the riverside path through four more gates and, as you approach the next bridlegate, turn left up steps to follow an old route through a wood. At the junction with Washings Lane, ignore the left turning and continue uphill, bearing right, to join Birches Road. Turn right here and follow the road towards St Mary's church.

Turn left at the church and follow the road south, with Church Hill Common to your right, ignoring turnings to the right. As the road swings right, cross a stone stile on the left by a signpost and walk down the path, going through a gate. Continue, using a stile and bridlegate to go through a paddock and reach a lane.

At the bottom of the lane, cross Black Brook stream and take a stile ahead, ignoring a turning to the left. Go up the field to cross another stile on to a road. Cross over and continue on a path through holly bushes to a stile. Cross and turn right up the road. Bear left at a road junction and, as the road swings right, leave it via a stone stile on the left into a field. Go straight ahead, and after another stone stile, turn right up a lane to reach the Bush Inn.

Continue past the Bush to join a narrow minor road, Lone Lane, and turn left. This lane descends all the way to the Boat.

② Tintern
The Anchor

The cosy lounge of this busy pub is dominated by a giant stone cider press, though it is not responsible for the Gaymer's Olde English at the bar. The pub is directly opposite the entrance to Tintern Abbey, and its stone buildings are quite in keeping with the scene. The separate restaurant room used to be the waiting room for a river ferry, now long gone. The warm bar area, with exposed stone walls, beams and small leaded windows is a welcoming place on a chilly day. When the sun shines, though, the place to be is in the pleasant beer garden.

The Anchor makes the most of its location, with the bar menu listing, among others, the Papal Edict (lasagne), Pilgrim's Progress (home-made soup) and Abbot's Delight (gammon steak). Children might opt for a Friar Tuck (burger in a bap) from their own Novices' menu. There are also chalked up specials like rabbit casserole, and everything is attractively presented and reasonably priced. At the bar you will find Tetley and Flowers Original real ale, plus Guinness and a range of keg beers and lagers.

Telephone: 0291 689207.

How to get there: The Anchor is opposite the abbey entrance in Tintern, off the A466 about 5 miles north of Chepstow.

9

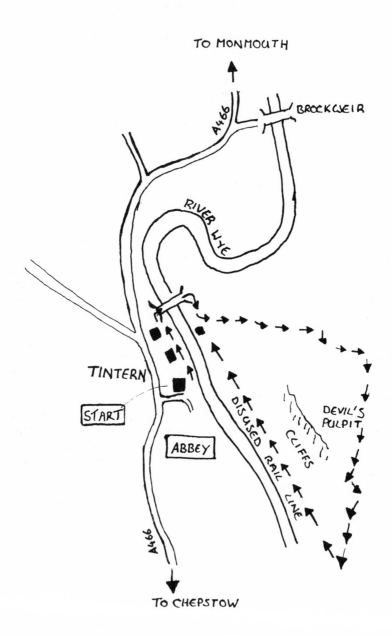

TO MONMOUTH

A466

BROCKWEIR

RIVER WYE

TINTERN

START

ABBEY

DISUSED RAIL LINE

CLIFFS

DEVIL'S PULPIT

A466

TO CHEPSTOW

Parking: There are large car parking areas (free) nearby.

Length of the walk: 4½ miles. Map: OS Landranger series 162 Gloucester and Forest of Dean area (GR 533002).

A wonderful walk in an area renowned for its scenic beauty which also allows a visit to the evocative remains of Tintern Abbey. While the pub is in Wales, the bulk of the route is actually in England but given that it follows in part Offa's Dyke, the 8th century boundary between English Mercia and Wales, we can overlook this. In any case, the finest views are Welsh! The popular circuit involves some quite steep ascents and descents.

The Walk

With the Wye to your right, follow the signposted path from the abbey entrance, turning left to the main road. Turn right for 100 yards, then right again to cross the footbridge over the river and into England.

Swing right along a waymarked track, then turn left up a steep, cobbled path. Where the track forks, take the right-hand option and go right again at another junction. Soon afterwards turn left, climbing a rough path which becomes surfaced. At a fork in the track bear right and, very shortly, go up steps to a forestry track.

Turn right, then left (waymarked) to climb to a signpost, where you take the right turn. You are now on the Offa's Dyke path and to the left can be seen a good section of the earthwork. The clear path continues beside and then atop the dyke. A sharp right turn brings you to the Devil's Pulpit, a pillar of limestone just below the path, overlooking the Wye and the abbey.

Carry on for about 20 minutes until your reach a path junction. Take a sharp right turn to drop down to another track. Turn left and, after 100 yards or so, look for a path to the right which descends to a forestry track junction. Continue down and keep to the track as it swings right to descend to the old railway line.

Turn right at the line and follow the path as it tracks the curve of the river back to the footbridge. From the bridge, reverse your steps to the pub.

3 Magor
The Wheatsheaf Inn

This attractive, whitewashed inn is in the heart of the quiet village of Magor, near the church and square – and hard by the M4 motorway, though that is hard to believe. A popular local, it is a friendly, roomy place and is used as a base for a number of walks in the area.

A restaurant area is divided from the large, comfortable lounge by an impressive fireplace and there is also a separate bar, the same menu applying throughout. The menu specialises in steaks, though not exclusively, and aims to offer value for money with substantial and filling meals, such as steak and ale pie. This hale and hearty approach is in keeping with the good selection of real ales – Flowers Original, Bass, Marston's Pedigree, Boddingtons and Wadworth 6X – as well as the usual keg choice. The pub has a beer garden at the rear and offers accommodation – ring for details.

Telephone: 0633 880608.

How to get there: The pub is in the centre of Magor village, which is on the B4245, east of Newport.

Parking: There is a pub car park as well as parking near the church.

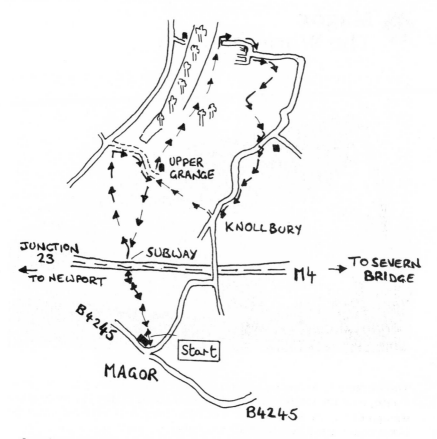

Length of the walk: About 3½ miles. Map: OS Landranger series 171 Cardiff, Newport and surrounding area (GR 425874).

An attractive countryside circuit in an area rich in history. Grange Farm was once owned by the monks of Tintern Abbey, and the St Brides valley, north of the motorway, is a designated Special Landscape Area.

The Walk

From the pub, turn left at the car park and go past a garage yard, once the site of a millpond which powered a saw mill. Go across the road and then a stream and turn left. Continue along the stream bank to a subway beneath the M4, crossing a stile.

Go under the subway and continue ahead, bearing slightly right from the stream. Go over a stile beside a field gate and continue beside the hedge to reach a minor road at a junction with a lane leading to

Upper Grange. Turn right up the lane and continue past the farmhouse. Turn left into the farmyard past the old farmhouse, and go through a gate into a field. Head straight on to reach a path which runs beside Grange Wood.

Continue to the right of the trees to reach a gate and a minor road (Common-y-Coed). Turn to the right down the lane, bearing right then left past White Hall Farm. Ignore a stile to the left. Instead, take a gate to the right just beyond the stile and head for the heap of stone in the middle of the field. Turn right and descend to a gate. Continue left over a stile and cross the field to a minor road near a three-way junction.

Turn to the right along the road and cross a stile on your left. Go right, up the hill, to meet the same road at a gate, then turn left down the road to a junction by a telephone box. Turn right to cross a gate, signposted to Upper Grange. With the hedge on your right, go ahead, crossing a stile and another field to a gateway. Do not go through, but turn left and walk beside the hedge to a copse. Turn right, along a gap between the wood and rough ground. Drop down the hill to a stile before the M4. Here you rejoin the path you started on. Return on the stream bank, turning right at the road to the pub.

4 Raglan
The Beaufort Arms Hotel

Exposed Tudor beams and timbers in the comfortable Castle country bar and Raglan lounge provide the link between this attractively modernised hotel, its 15th century past and darker days. Roundhead soldiers probably refreshed themselves here during the Civil War siege of Raglan Castle in 1646. Legend has it that a tunnel connects the pub to the castle – no doubt the soldiers who laboriously demolished the castle's Great Tower with pickaxes would have loved to have found it!

Refreshments today include Courage Directors and Best, Wadworth 6X and guest ales, and widely recommended food. In the restaurant, as well as eating à la carte, a three-course table d'hôte menu is available, with main courses such as sirloin of beef in red wine and peppercorns, and lamb cutlets in cider and redcurrant sauce. In the bar, vegetarian meals are among the 30 dishes offered, which include home-made soup, mussels provençale and fresh sardines. There is a patio area at the front and the hotel has 10 letting bedrooms, if you would like a longer stay.

Telephone: 0291 690412.

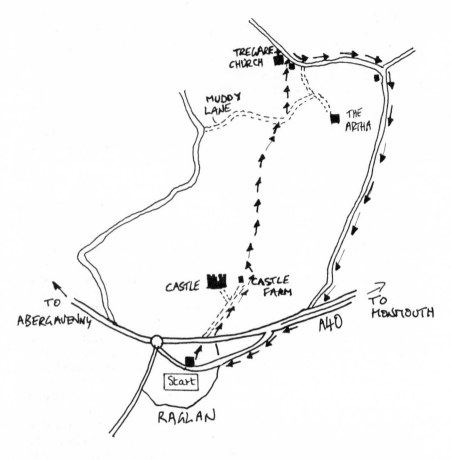

How to get there: Raglan is signposted from the A40, between Monmouth and Abergavenny. The hotel is in the centre of the village.

Parking: There is a car park beside the hotel and roadside parking in the village.

Length of the walk: 4 miles. Map: OS Landranger series 161 Abergavenny and the Black Mountains (GR 414076).

A lovely walk, across fields and along hedge-lined quiet lanes, with fine views — especially of Raglan Castle. You go past Tregare church (worth a detour) and can stop to search for the 1712 tombstone of Isaac and Elizabeth Williams of the Artha, a house you pass on the walk.

The Walk

Turn left from the car park and left again down Castle Street. Follow the road around until a gap in the wall leads to the dual carriageway. Cross carefully and head up the lane opposite, signposted to the castle.

Carry on up the lane past the castle entrance (a visit is highly recommended if you have time) and, well before you reach a farm, cross a stile to the right. Keep to the top edge of the fields, crossing stiles with yellow waymarks, until you swing round to the left to meet a rough lane leading back to the farm. Cross directly over into another field. Aim diagonally right across the next field, keeping to the left of what looks an old pillbox on the brow ahead of you. A marker post should help guide you to a stile to your right below you. Look back for a stunning view of the castle.

Follow a clear path across the next field, crossing a shallow stream, then another field. In the far corner of the field, before reaching a pond in a thicket, cross a stile to the right. Follow the perimeter of the field to a gateway in the top left-hand corner. Turn left and follow the hedge line to another stile. Cross it into a green lane and turn right, then leave it via an old gate on your left. Head straight across the field to another gate. Go to the right of a sunken lane and some ruined buildings, then cross an open pasture with Tregare church ahead of you.

Bear right as you approach the church, to a gate onto the main road. A detour to the left to the churchyard is worthwhile. Retrace your steps and carry on down the lane, passing a house, Silver Birches, on your right. At a road junction by a house, take the right turn, signposted 'Raglan', and descend easily, with fine views of Raglan Castle over the fields to your right.

This lane descends to reach the dual carriageway at a complex junction – it is easy to cross in stages, but take care. Cross over and turn right along the signposted slip road to Raglan. After a short stretch without pavement, you are off the road all the way back to the hotel.

⑤ Llantilio Crossenny
The Hostry Inn

You are not likely just to stumble upon the Hostry, tucked away in a tiny village in Gwent's rural emptiness, but it is well worth a special visit. A pub since 1459, it retains the comfortable, no-frills feel of a country local. The stone walls, simple furnishings and open fireplace are all the genuine articles and the owners have not forgotten what else makes a pub – good beer and food.

All meals, except things like scampi, are prepared on the premises and there is a particularly impressive choice of vegetarian food, such as baked dishes of cashew and parsnip, mushroom and broccoli or celery, walnut and apple. Grilled salmon fillets, caught locally, are popular and other options include beef and tomato casserole and steak braised in red wine. The lunchtime menu contains slightly fewer items, but it includes such substantial snacks as faggots, peas and wholemeal bread and veggie lasagne. A three-course lunch is available on Sunday. The real ales are Wye Valley Brewery Hereford Bitter and Brew 69, plus guest beers.

There is a good beer garden and a large hall, used for functions, can become an informal family room if space is pressing. Although the Hostry does not offer beds, accommodation can be arranged in local

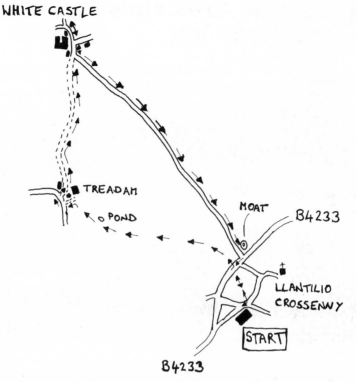

WHITE CASTLE

TREADAM

o POND

MOAT

B4233

LLANTILIO CROSSENWY

START

B4233

farmhouses, with the farmer collecting guests from the pub when they've been sufficiently fed and watered – a service popular with walkers tackling the Offa's Dyke Path, which runs past.
Telephone: 060 085 278.

How to get there: The Hostry is in the village of Llantilio Crossenny, just off the B4233 between Monmouth and Abergavenny.

Parking: The pub has a fair-sized car park, and there is limited roadside parking elsewhere.

Length of the walk: About 4½ miles. Map: OS Landranger series 161 Abergavenny and the Black Mountains (GR 396146).

An attractive walk in a historic area, partly on the Offa's Dyke long distance footpath. The walk hinges on White Castle – an atmospheric stronghold isolated on a hilltop – one of a trio of castles (now linked by a waymarked footpath) which originally formed defences for the Norman Lords Marcher.

The Walk

With your back to the pub car park, turn right and walk down the road. Go left through a metal kissing-gate, signposted 'Offa's Dyke Path'. Walk directly across a field to a stile opposite and continue, trending rightwards, to a roadside metal kissing-gate. Cross the road and the stile almost opposite and follow a reasonably clear path heading directly across a field, passing a large oak to your right.

Cross another stile and go directly across the next field, underneath power cables, aiming for a section of wooden fencing in the hedge ahead, where there is a stile. Continue in the same direction, across the centre of the field, to another stile you can see in the hedge ahead. Carry on, uphill now, across another field, aiming for a line of cables on the skyline. As you reach the brow of the hill, passing beneath the cables, you will see a stile in front of a copse. Cross and continue, with the trees on your right, to approach Great Treadam Farm.

Go through a gateway and turn sharp left, descending to a lane where you turn right, passing below the fine house on your right. Just beyond the house, turn right up a lane past some houses, signposted 'Offa's Dyke Path'. This rough-surfaced track climbs steadily all the way towards White Castle, which eventually comes into view straight ahead. As you approach a house at the end of the track, note the lane dropping rightwards almost back on yourself – this is the road back to the pub. To visit the impressive castle, carry straight on in front of houses to swing leftwards to the entrance gate. Retrace your steps to the lane you noted earlier, ignoring another lane with a 'Three Castles Path' signpost beside it.

Go down the lane, which descends quite sharply to begin with, and follow it all the way back to the B4233 near Llantilio Crossenny in about 30 minutes. As you approach the road, note a historic monument signpost and stile to the left. This refers to The Old Court, a moated site occupied in the 13th and 14th centuries, possibly by a manor house belonging to the Bishops of Llandaff. It later formed part of a deer park created by the Herbert family, probably in use until the siege of Raglan Castle in the English Civil War. Llandaff Cathedral and Raglan Castle are visited by other walks in this book. All that is left within the reed-lined moat is a flat patch of ground – worth a quick look, though.

Back on the lane, turn right along the B4233, and a little way past the road signpost for 'The Hostry' reach a kissing-gate on the left, the one you used on the way out. Retrace your steps across the fields and stiles to the kissing-gate near the pub.

6 Usk
The Nag's Head

Named after the river renowned for its salmon fishing which runs beside, the ancient borough of Usk is an attractive place, with a pub seemingly at every turn. Set unobtrusively in the large square, the Nag's Head is very much part of the local scene, and a fine place to sample the famous fish.

Timber beams, horse brasses, harnesses and assorted agricultural tools are not the result of an interior designer's whim here. This is a traditional village inn, comfortable and welcoming. It is Egon Ronay recommended and has a formidable reputation for food. There are popular specials, such as half duck in Cointreau, venison pie and available only during their season, fresh Usk salmon and local pheasant cooked in port. Snails in garlic butter and freshly grilled sardines are among the regular starters, while main courses include home-made rabbit pie and chicken in red wine. Vegetarians have a tempting choice, including Glamorgan sausage, made of cheese and leeks, and pancakes filled with mushrooms, broccoli and leeks. At the bar, the beer choice includes Buckley's Best and Flowers Original, and if all this food and drink is too much for you, you do not have to budge – the inn offers five twin-bedded rooms for overnight accommodation.

Telephone: 0291 672820.

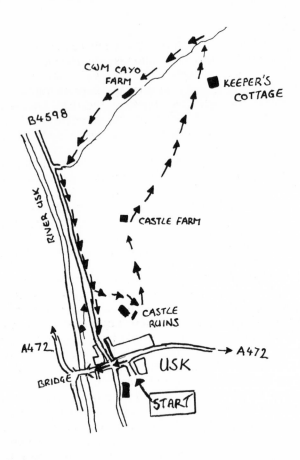

How to get there: The pub is in Twyn Square in the centre of Usk on the A472, east of Pontypool.

Parking: The pub has no car park but there is parking in the square plus a large car park, signposted around the corner.

Length of the walk: 4 miles. Map: OS Landranger series 171 Cardiff, Newport and surrounding area (GR 377008).

A lovely walk with fine scenery, and full of interest almost as soon as you leave the main road. As you pass the ruins of Usk Castle, ponder the fact that 1,500 Welshmen were killed in the fields near Castle Farm when Gruffyd, son of Owain Glyndwr, was defeated in 1405.

The Walk

With your back to the pub, turn left and left again into the main street. Continue down the main street and take the riverside footpath to the right of the bridge, signposted 'Conigar Walk'. Ignore a right fork in the path, and carry straight on until the path swings away from the river to emerge through a metal gate on the Usk–Abergavenny road. Turn left towards an old railway bridge over the road. Immediately before the bridge cross the road and take a track climbing right, signposted 'Gwehelog'.

Keep right, leaving the main track, to follow a rising path with a wooden fence on your right. Continue to climb and shortly the remains of Usk Castle can be seen, grimly defying the vegetation. Descend until you reach the main gates to Castle House on your right. Directly opposite them is a five-bar gate. Turn left through it and follow a good track, rising across pasture. The track becomes a lane and when you reach Castle Farm on your left, take the right-hand fork, waymarked with a yellow arrow.

Continue through another gate on a clear path with a hedge on your left. Pleasant views open out on the left and right, helped by a closely trimmed hedge when I walked it – thank you, farmer! The path heads towards mature woodland and enters it by a stile. Ignore a path to the right and stick to the main track. Pass a large pond on the left, staying on the main track, and soon reach a six-bar gate and stile, giving entry to a field. The path continues with the wood to your left. Ignore the first gate on your left, but re-enter the wood at the second, which has a sign on it, 'Kittybeech Road', and a yellow arrow waymark.

Go through the woods with coppiced trees to your left, then descend beneath giant broadleaved trees. Go directly ahead at a track crossroads and you soon cross a small stream, where a railway sleeper is an effective bridge. Once across the stream, turn sharp left, passing a small gate on your right. Go through another gate (yellow waymark) and carry on, keeping the fence and stream on your left. You shortly reach a farm track which leads through Cwm Cayo Farm. Continue along this track, which soon bends to the right, past a house on your right, ignoring another track coming in from the left, and descend to the Usk–Abergavenny road.

Cross the road (take care) and turn left. After a few yards there is access on your right to a pleasant riverside path. Turn left to keep the river on your right and the path soon climbs to rejoin the road. Turn right at the road to continue into Usk. Turn left beyond the Three Salmons Hotel. Twyn Square and the Nag's Head is ahead to the right.

7 Llandegveth
The Farmer's Arms

The village of Llandegveth (or Llandegfedd), set in beautiful countryside to the south of the reservoir of the same name, consisted originally of two large houses – Cwrt Perrott and Waun-y-Pwll – some cottages and a church. Despite the attractions of the place, it is not much more than that now – although an interesting feature is Cwrt Perrott Cottages, built by a Quaker owner of one of the big houses as part of 'The Scheme' to provide homes and work for out-of-work miners.

The Farmer's Arms is a friendly village pub, well known to ramblers – the local group frequently uses it as a starting point. The split-level lounge is attractive and comfortable, and there is a separate cosy restaurant, which families may use if they wish, beyond a rustic bar with ceiling beams. Outside is a small patio area with tables, and sunshades for warmer days.

Food is plentiful and good value, the three-course Sunday lunch – for example Florida cocktail with sherry, roast lamb, cheese and biscuits – being particularly popular. Bar meals include battered calamari rings, home-made steak and kidney pie and vegetarian options, like a vegetable platter consisting of crispy coated sweetcorn,

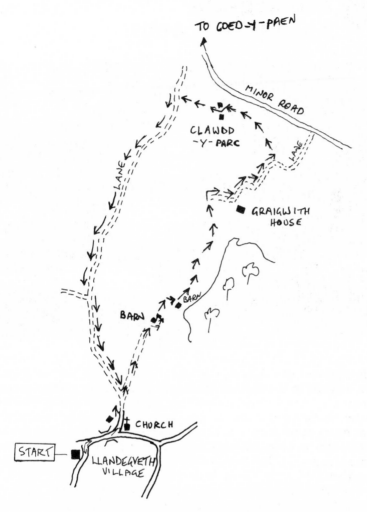

TO COED-Y-PAEN

MINOR ROAD

CLAWDD -Y- PARC

LANE

LANE

GRAIGWITH HOUSE

BARN

BARN

CHURCH

START — LLANDEGVETH VILLAGE

cauliflower, courgettes, mushrooms and Brie wedge. Brains Bitter and Dark (mild) are on offer, as well as draught Worthington Best and Murphy's, plus lagers and ciders.

Telephone: 0633 450244.

How to get there: The Farmer's Arms is on the western fringe of the small village of Llandegveth, on a minor road south-east of Pontypool and north of Caerleon. The village is episodically signposted and the OS map comes in handy.

25

Parking: The pub has two car parks.

Length of the walk: 4 miles. Map: OS Landranger series 171 Cardiff, Newport and surrounding area (GR 335957).

An excellent rural circuit almost entirely on tracks. The route includes a lovely valley bridleway and there are superb views from the highest point at 600 ft to the Bristol Channel and beyond.

The Walk

Turn left from the pub car park and follow the road around to the right, crossing a road bridge. Turn sharp left, then go to the right up a rough track with the church on your right, soon passing between farm buildings. Take the gate ahead, waymarked with a blue arrow, ignoring the lane to your left.

As you approach a barn take the gate to the right of the track and head for the building, all that remains of a farm, turning right then left to skirt it. At the far corner, cross directly over the field to a gate with a waymark – a barn with a galvanised roof, beyond it, is a useful target.

Go through the gate and descend to cross a stream, going through another gate on its far side. Head towards the barn and another gate, then follow a lovely bridleway with a fence and hedge on your right. At the right time of year this area is alive with pheasants.

After a gate turn right and descend a track towards Graigwith House, passing to the left of the fine building. The track swings left then right, crossing a stream, then climbs left. As it begins to swing rightwards again, keep your eyes peeled to your left for a stile. If you miss it and reach a gate at a copse, you have gone too far and the best bet is to turn around, head to the right towards the hedge on a bank and follow it until you find the stile. Cross the stile and follow a path, swinging around towards a farm on the skyline. Aim for the right-hand house and go through a waymarked metal gate, then another, to emerge in an open field. Go up the left side of the field, then trend diagonally rightwards to a stile in the middle of the top hedge.

Cross a sunken path to a stile opposite, then turn left. The path descends alongside the sunken lane, crossing stiles, until eventually it joins it at a junction of lanes. Take the left-hand lane, descending to the farm you passed at the start. Retrace your steps to the pub.

8 Llanvihangel Crucorney
The Skirrid Inn

Few pubs can match the past of the Skirrid Inn – and I do not just mean its age. The inn dates back to 1110, so its claim to be the oldest in Wales is a strong one, but it is its lurid history, an accumulation of fact and legend detailed in a leaflet available at the pub, which captures the imagination. The pub was for centuries a court-house and up to 180 people are believed to have been hanged on the premises between the 12th and 17th centuries. A beam at the bottom of the stairs with scorch and drag marks is thought to have been the scaffold. Ancient beams, exposed stone walls, flagged floors and a roaring open fire in an immense bar-room fireplace in winter provide an atmospheric connection to those dark days. All is peace now, with even the traffic which used to rumble past the roadside pub diverted well clear of the village on a bypass.

For all its gory connections, the Skirrid is a cheery, welcoming place with a reputation for good food. The menu changes virtually every day, using fresh local produce to create imaginative choices, and is served in both the bar and the small, wood-panelled restaurant. Among the options on the board may be vegetable soup, wild rabbit in white wine, cream, garlic and green peppercorn sauce, aubergine, pepper and cheese bake, local lamb chops and whole stuffed Crucorney trout. An Ushers pub, it offers the brewery's Founders and Best real ales. It is still a genuine inn, with three double bedrooms, and has a beer garden at the rear. Children are welcome in the restaurant.

Telephone: 0873 890258.

How to get there: The small village is signposted from the A465 which bypasses it about 6 miles north of Abergavenny. The pub is near a filling station and cannot be missed.

Parking: The pub has a large car park, reached through an arch. The landlord is happy for walkers to leave cars, providing they will be customers – a courtesy call in the pub to say you will be back is a good idea.

Length of the walk: About 5 miles. Maps: OS Landranger series 161 Abergavenny and the Black Mountains, or OS Outdoor Leisure sheet 13 Brecon Beacons National Park Eastern Area (GR 325206).

Comparisons with the Matterhorn, which some writers have made, are stretching the point, but the Skirrid looks every inch a mountain despite its modest 1,594 ft height. This route up the Holy Mountain (a chapel once stood on it) is no pushover but fit and active walkers will love it. The descent, in particular, is steep and not recommended for young children. The reward for the effort is the quite exceptional views.

The Walk

With your back to the front of the pub, turn right and walk down the road to the churchyard. Cross the road and go left down a lane opposite the church gate to the A465. Take care crossing this busy road and continue down a lane opposite. This swings right, passing Llanvihangel Court, an impressive pile dating back to Tudor times, and the wooden skeleton of an old barn to the left.

Continue along the lane between stone walls, ignoring a signpost for the Skirrid to the right. Cross a stile beside a double gate and carry on between fencing. You soon come to a stream which can be hopped across, but mud is unavoidable on the deeply rutted track. A barrier formed by a gate and fallen tree is best rounded to the right.

Continue up the sunken lane to reach a hay feed unit by a set of gates. Cross the left-hand gate and for a while follow the better track beside the lane, which is now a proper stream bed. After a couple of minutes look out for a stile on the right of the stream. Cross it and turn left up the field beside the fence. Go over a stile and carry on with the fence to the left.

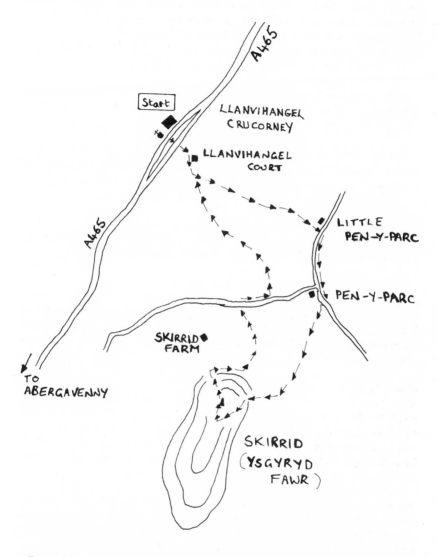

By a derelict cottage cross a stile on your left and turn right up a sunken lane. If this is blocked, escape into the field on the left. Walk up beside the lane to cross a stile by a gate and emerge on a lane, where you turn right. The Skirrid is now ahead.

Ignore a road turning to the right and, about 200 yards beyond it, take a track off the road to the right leading to a gate and wood fence pen. Hop over the gate and, bearing right, cross the wooden fence into a field. Head up the field, with a sunken lane to the right. At the end of the gully, carry on upwards with a fence to the right. Continue uphill, crossing fields, until you approach the lower boundary fence of the top field and bear slightly left from the fence to a gate. Head on up, bearing left to cross a stile in the top boundary fence.

Go straight ahead to join a clear track climbing diagonally leftwards, an ancient pilgrims' path. Take it steadily here, as the path climbs steeply. Pause frequently to admire the views behind you – always a good excuse. Quite soon you emerge on the narrow summit ridge, near hollows which offer protection on a windy day. Turn right to reach the summit pillar and enjoy the fantastic views, dominated by the distinctive shape of the Sugarloaf hill to the left.

From the summit take the clear, narrow path descending to the left. Take care here as you soon approach a rocky drop. Bear right, keeping well clear of dodgy edges, and drop very steeply on grass, straight downwards, using small flatter patches and path traces. The steep route down is actually well walked and quite safe, as long as you take your time. A guide to the line of descent is to aim for a group of tin barns below you.

On more level ground, turn right when you hit an unmistakeable path running around the base of the mountain. Continue on the track until you reach a gate on the left and go through the waymarked wooden latch gate beside it.

Go straight down the field, keeping a ditch to your left. Cross a stile ahead of you and carry on, with the gully to your left. At the bottom left corner of the field, cross a stile to the left by a gate and head for a stile to the right of an old barn. Carry on down an obvious path to cross a stile near a house and emerge on a lane. Turn right and after about five minutes along the lane take a stile on the left just before a house, signposted 'Crucorney 2 kms'.

Go straight down fields with the fence on your right, passing through a gap in a hedge. Carry on down with a ravine on the right, crossing another stile. Towards the bottom end of this field bear left to cross a stile into trees. Go directly through the small wood to cross a small footbridge, and clamber up and over yet another stile. Bear left across the middle of this field, aiming for the small, tattered clump of trees nearest you. Just beyond the trees reach the top left corner of a fenced enclosure and go straight on with the top fence on your right. Carry on, crossing stiles and following the fence, towards a tin barn. Cross a stile to the right of the tin building and turn left up the lane – this is the one you used at the beginning. Follow it past Llanvihangel Court, carefully cross the main road again and retrace your steps to the pub.

Upper Llanover
The Goose and Cuckoo

At the end of the road, the pub and a couple of homes sit high on the eastern flanks of a finger of high ground thrusting towards Abergavenny which culminates in the Blorenge – a popular target for walkers.

It seems that as many customers arrive on foot or mountain bike as by car at this superbly situated pub. That is not surprising as it is tricky to find by road. It is worth the effort, though, if only for the sensational view to the south from the small side room the owners call their 'conference facility', with tongues firmly in cheeks. Simply furnished with no frills, the pub is unpretentious and homely. Muddy boots will not raise any eyebrows and the stove burning in the impressive fireplace in winter adds to the warm welcome from the owners. Customers prove to be pretty loyal, a Nepalese from Kathmandu being a regular, if not frequent, visitor.

The food is hearty, wholesome and good value. Vegetarian dishes are a speciality, all made freshly and using ingredients according to season. Thirteen-bean soup with home-made bread is a popular choice and other dishes include mushroom lasagne and leek coustarde. Real

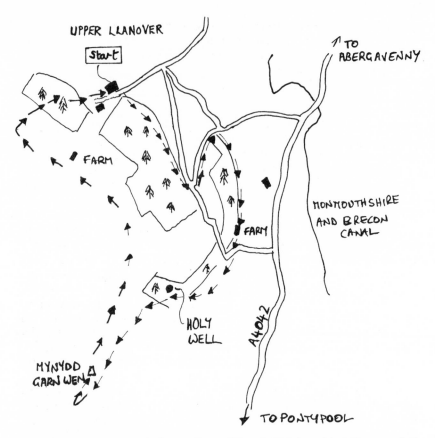

UPPER LLANOVER

Start

FARM

FARM

HOLY WELL

MYNYDD GARN WEN

↗ TO ABERGAVENNY

MONMOUTHSHIRE AND BRECON CANAL

A4042

TO PONTYPOOL

ales include Wadworth 6X, Bullmastiff and Old Speckled Hen, and if you fancy something stronger we counted 23 malt whiskies behind the bar.
Telephone: 0873 880277.

How to get there: Leave the A4042 about 3½ miles south of Abergavenny, signposted 'Upper Llanover'. Bear left at a fork, then continue on the minor road to find the pub on the left.

Parking: The car park is adjacent, and there is an overflow area nearly opposite (which can be very muddy).

Length of the walk: 6 miles. Maps: OS Landranger series 161 Abergavenny and the Black Mountains, plus a small section on sheet 171, Cardiff, Newport and surrounding area (GR 292074).

Excellent views are the reward from this fairly strenuous walk which also visits Holy Well — a spring with religious connections. It is not difficult, but involves an exposed ridge so is best reserved for fine days with good visibility. The route can be soggy in places so good footwear is essential.

The Walk

With your back to the pub, turn left down the road, then right on a track into forestry. Keep on this path, ignoring the temptation to stray on to tracks to the right. At a rough road turn left to reach a tarmac road and go straight on down to eventually reach a junction.

Turn right up a short stretch of metalled road and go through a gate to follow a track up through trees. Keep to the track on the boundary of the forest to reach a stile. Go ahead, still on the forest edge, to pass Pen-y-stair Farm, where there is a pottery.

Go ahead, ignoring a track on your right and the left turn of the road. After about 250 yards take the right fork before a drive to a cottage. After a stile trend rightwards across a field to reach another stile into the woods. Climb steadily, with a stream to your left. Just after the next stile the Holy Well is to the right.

Keep climbing, crossing a stile and a tiny stone footbridge to another stile. Ignore the path (waymarked) to the left and instead climb sharply ahead through bracken, between trees. Turn left when you reach a track and carry on for about ½ mile, ignoring left forks. At a junction of several tracks near a wall turn sharp right and climb to the trig point on Mynydd Garn Wen.

After a pause to catch breath, continue northwards on grassy paths to eventually pass a whitewashed farmhouse to your right. About 500 yards beyond the farm descend rightwards between walls to reach a gate. Go through, and continue descending. Cross a broad forest road and continue to a metalled road which is followed down to the pub.

10 Rogerstone
The Rising Sun

A visitor centre and picnic site have been developed above the great flight of 14 locks which once raised and lowered barges 168 ft in ½ mile on the western arm of the Monmouthshire Canal. The disused locks and related ponds and weirs remain an impressive feat of engineering. The Rising Sun, in an outlying part of Newport, is just across the road from the canal and a few minutes' walk from the visitor centre.

A large balcony with panoramic plate-glass windows is a striking feature of this large, well-furnished hotel, which is set back off the road. The scene can also be enjoyed from a good beer garden and play area with climbing frame. Almost as tempting as the view is the impressive tower of desserts which catches the eye beside the busy servery counter. Bar meals in this well-run and popular establishment include beef in red wine, glazed lamb cutlets and chicken in mushroom cream, all with a good choice of vegetables. Generous salads are also available and children's favourites, like beefburgers or fish fingers, are good value. The restaurant serves a wide selection of dishes, featuring steaks, fish and chicken. Bass, John Smith's and Courage Best are among the beers and Guinness and Beamish are also at the bar, beside cider and a wide range of lagers. The hotel has five bedrooms and has been awarded three crowns by the Welsh Tourist Board.

Telephone: 0633 895126.

How to get there: Rogerstone lies to the west of Newport and can be easily reached via junction 27 of the M4, signposted High Cross. Follow signposts for Fourteen Locks Canal Centre, but continue past the right-hand turn sign. The Rising Sun is a short distance further, to the left.

Parking: The pub has a large car park. There is some on-road parking nearby, or cars may be left at the canal centre car park.

Length of the walk: 3½ miles. Map: OS Landranger series 171 Cardiff, Newport and surrounding area (GR 276885).

A chance to visit the impressive flight of Fourteen Locks on the Monmouthshire and Brecon Canal, and its visitor centre, plus great views from the elevated Ridgeway.

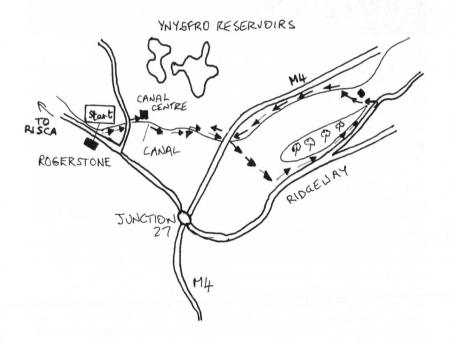

The Walk

Cross the road from the pub entrance, with great care, to a small gap in the wall opposite, the entry to the canal towpath. Turn right and, after 150 yards or so, come to a low barrier beside a bridge. Cross the bridge and bear right to the visitor centre car park.

Go to the other side of the canal and turn left down the towpath. Cross the canal at a bridge by Pensarn Cottage, turn right and walk down to where the path passes under the M4 motorway. According to the visitor centre, what takes about 15 minutes on foot used to take barges some two hours.

Beyond the motorway subway, bear left, pass a cottage and go right, over a bridge, to reach a kissing-gate. Go through and head directly up through fields (gates and stile) to reach the path alongside the Ridgeway road overlooking the canal and Ynysfro reservoirs.

Turn left and walk along the Ridgeway, bearing left at a fork from the main road into Allt-yr-yn View. Go past a hospital and take a lane on your left with a footpath sign. Descend, passing Strawberry Farm to the right, to the canal. Cross a bridge and turn left to follow the towpath back to the subway and on to the visitor centre, then on back to the gap in the wall. Take care when crossing back to the pub as there is no pavement beside the wall.

11 Crickhowell
The Bear Hotel

An excellent base for exploring the splendid Black Mountains, the small market town of Crickhowell is well worth a visit in its own right. The much-photographed multi-arched stone bridge over the Usk is crossed on the walk and it is approached via the steep Bridge Street – almost entirely 18th century.

The Bear Hotel, an old coaching inn, faces the town square and is a rare thing. It is a hotel with 30 rooms, some with jacuzzis, yet retains the atmosphere of a genuine, unpretentious country hostelry. Written up as far afield as in the *New York Times*, and laden with accolades, it is a well-known port of call for locals and travellers alike and deservedly so.

The spacious, darkly furnished lounge bar features a timbered ceiling and huge open fireplace, with furniture including rustic chairs and comfy sofa. It is a large place, with separate award-winning restaurants, a family room where children are welcome and an enclosed courtyard. The bar menu emphasises local produce – the lamb is supplied by a barmaid – and is both plentiful and reasonably priced. Prawns tossed in garlic mayonnaise, salmon fish-cakes, chicken, ham and onion pie, grilled lamb cutlets with rosemary and grilled bacon

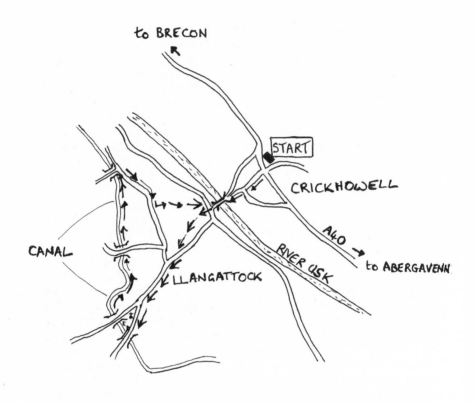

with cockle and laverbread cakes, for example, are among the choices. Beer fans, too, are well catered for with Ruddles County, Ruddles Best, Bass and Webster's Yorkshire Bitter.

Telephone: 0873 810408.

How to get there: The Bear is in the centre of Crickhowell, reached by the A40 north-west of Abergavenny.

Parking: The hotel has limited parking space. It may be better to use the large public car park, well signposted nearby.

Length of the walk: About 3 miles. Map: OS Landranger series 161 Abergavenny and the Black Mountains (GR 217184).

An easy but interesting walk offering good views of this beautiful part of the world and focused on a charming canal towpath, once a hive of industry.

The Walk

With your back to the front of the pub, cross the road and walk ahead down High Street. Bear right when the road splits and continue down to reach the town's attractive arched bridge.

On the far side cross (carefully) the main road and go through a kissing-gate opposite the bridge to a metalled path. Pass a graveyard to the left and continue through another gate. At a path junction ignore the right-hand turn over a footbridge and follow the left fork through a gate into an alley.

The alley turns sharp left to emerge suddenly on to a road with no pavement – take care with children. Turn right up the street and continue uphill, ignoring a right turn, until you reach a large stone church, Bethesda Congregational. Take the road to the left of the church and after about 150 yards reach a bridge over the Monmouthshire and Brecon Canal. Don't cross but use projecting stones near a footpath signpost to climb the left-hand wall and descend to the towpath – it is easier than it looks.

Turn right under the bridge. Just beyond a second bridge note the limekilns of Llangattock Wharf on the far side of the canal. Continue along the towpath, possibly muddy at this point, enjoying the views to the right. Go below another stone bridge, then under a wooden footbridge. At the next stone bridge, with number 118 on the arch, leave the towpath in front of it to reach a lane. Turn right, dropping quite steeply, to a road junction.

Turn right with good views to the left, of the mountains looming above Crickhowell. After a couple of minutes turn left down a lane (footpath signpost), passing houses on your left. Swing right along the lane to reach a kissing-gate to the left of a barn. Go through and follow the surfaced path across a field, swinging left to another kissing-gate and the main road. Crickhowell Bridge is a few yards to the right. Cross over, turn right and retrace your steps uphill to High Street and the Bear.

Blackrock
12
The Drum and Monkey

The name of the inn, once a Chartist meeting place, is believed to be derived from hard industrial days. Children used to run along greasing the brake drums of the tram wheels. These youngsters, known as grease monkeys, worked on the drums – hence Drum and Monkey.

It is primarily a restaurant, though the lounge bar area, with thick walls, exposed stone and beams, is a cosy and friendly place to enjoy a meal and drink. The food is first class, with fish and seafood a speciality. Monkfish with crevette mousse in filo pastry with bisque sauce, and salmon topped with spinach mousse and baked in puff pastry with hollandaise sauce are examples of the unusual dishes on the board. Other lunchtime options include seafood pasta, and pasta with wild mushrooms, served with French bread. Boddingtons is the real ale at the small bar, plus lagers and Murphy's.

Telephone: 0873 831980.

How to get there: The Drum and Monkey can be seen on the north side of the A465 Heads of the Valleys road between Gilwern and Brynmawr – but there is no direct access. Instead, take the signposted exit to Blackrock, east of the pub and go left, following the minor road parallel to the A465 to reach the pub entrance on your left.

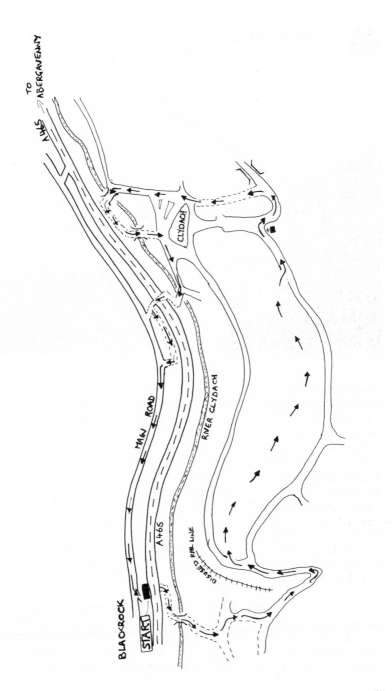

Parking: The inn has a large car park.

Length of the walk: About 4 miles. Map: OS Landranger series 161 Abergavenny and the Black Mountains (GR 215126).

A fascinating walk through an area rich in industrial and cultural heritage – now including a national nature reserve. The route involves steep climbs and descents and care should be taken to stay on footpaths, as old workings can be dangerous.

The Walk

Go through the signposted gate beside the inn and take the subway below the main road. Turn right over the stile and follow the path entering Cwm Clydach. Cross Devil's Bridge and carry straight on up, very steeply. At a junction turn left and then bear right. Ignore a track entrance on the right and continue left on the road.

Follow this road as it swings sharply around to the left. Below and to the left are the tunnels of a disused railway line. Pass a right turning to Llanelli Hill and take the next right, on to a track. Go along this track climbing right to a lane below a terrace. Turn left, passing other homes. Keep on the lane, bearing right, to cross a footbridge. Continue to a prominent hill fort, then descend rightwards and turn left on reaching a road, which leads to the Nazareth chapel on your right.

Take a footpath right, beyond the chapel, which passes Clydach station on your right, closed in 1958. As you approach Clydach Viaduct, take the footpath to the left and descend sharply, crossing a wooden bridge. Carry on down, to reach Station Road, and a car park and picnic area.

Turn left and then bear right to cross the river Clydach by Pant Glas Bridge, a railway bridge built in 1795. Turn left and walk beside the river to Smart's Bridge, to cross the Clydach again. Ahead of you now is the site of Clydach Ironworks. Closed in 1877, the works employed more than 1,350 people in 1841, including 133 children under 13.

Keep to the right of the works and, at the top of the incline, take the first turning right into the Dan-y-Coed estate, ignoring the road ahead which climbs the gorge. You pass some bungalows, bearing right, then turn right to cross a footbridge over the A465.

Climb the path, bearing right and then take the second sharp left on to a road. Pass a school to the left and, at a footpath signpost, turn right up a narrow track to emerge on a main road, formerly the 1812 Merthyr–Govilon turnpike road. Turn left on this quiet road and continue past the Rock and Fountain on the right to reach the Drum and Monkey below to the left.

Rudry
The Maenllwyd Inn

13

Up in the narrow lanes and wooded hillsides around Rudry village it is hard to believe you are just a few miles from Cardiff and Caerphilly. Long ago coal was worked here – the little craters on Rudry Common are the result – but now this is a delightful rural corner to explore and enjoy.

The attractive Maenllwyd Inn has been serving beer for more than 300 years, but the core of the building is even older. Originally a farm, it is believed to date back more than 450 years. Evidence of its past as a Welsh longhouse can be seen in the main lounge, where a stone staircase at one corner forms an interesting feature. Among the many tales surrounding the pub – including ghosts and hauntings – is one where a 'horde of bingeing, womanising mariners and smugglers were beaten back by locals from the Maenllwyd Inn armed with pitchforks'. Nowadays you will meet customers armed only with knives and forks.

Home-made bar meals include chicken and ham, and steak and kidney pies plus daily specials, of which local trout is a popular choice. The restaurant serves a good range of dishes with the emphasis on fish and steaks, though a starter of chicken samosa and spinach pakoras with sour cream and chive dip, followed by Chinese turkey steak is a spicy alternative. Beers include Theakston and Younger plus, unusually, Becks and Coors lagers on draught.

Telephone: 0222 882372.

How to get there: The straggling hamlet of Rudry lies in the centre of a tangle of minor roads and lanes north-east of Cardiff's Lisvane suburb and east of Caerphilly – the quickest way to get there depends very much on your starting point. To locate it on the map, find the A468 running from Newport to Caerphilly. At Lower Machen a minor road leads west to Draethen. Continue west beyond Draethen to find the pub at a crossroads.

Parking: There is a large parking area facing the pub, but the entrance to it is some distance west along the Rudry road. The car park approach road doubles back on itself to the pub. It is signposted from the crossroads.

Length of the walk: 5½ miles. Map: OS Landranger series 171 Cardiff, Newport and surrounding area (GR 201866).

This fine, energetic walk combines the heath of Rudry Common with delightful woodland and wonderful views from the ridge used for the return leg – part of the Ridgeway footpath.

The Walk

With your back to the pub, turn right along the road and take the first right turn down a lane. Descend quite steeply, passing Rudry chapel on your left to reach a road junction, with a school on your right. Keep left and shortly afterwards take a track to the left, signposted 'Ael-y-bryn'.

Pass the house to your left and enter the common, which is popular with horse-riders and sometimes quite muddy. The path soon draws level with a grey kissing-gate to the left. Ignore the gate and continue on the clear path through bracken, diverging from the hedge. Cross a quite marshy area to reach a T-junction of paths at the edge of a small wood.

Turn right and follow the path around the perimeter of the wood to reach a gate and stile. Ahead you can see the distinctive shape of Mynydd Rudry. Go over the stile, and the path follows the edge of the wood. To the right is a sea of bracken, while to the left the open woods form a good play area, having lots of attractive clearings. Cross another stile and follow the path through bracken.

A bench seat on the skyline ahead is a good marker for the large car

44

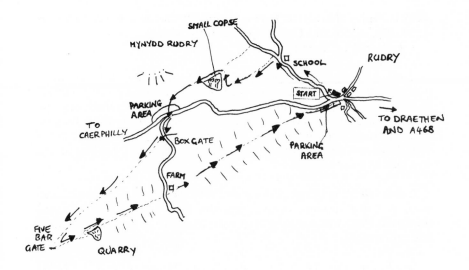

park which is the next target. Paths to the right lead to the top of Mynydd Rudry. Cross the minor road serving the car park, and take the metalled side road opposite it, climbing diagonally right. Pause to admire the view of Caerphilly Castle.

A box gate (to allow horses through) on the right leads into forestry. Follow a good path with open views – a good place to play 'Last of the Mohicans'. At a path junction, bear left, following a blue waymark on a post. Descend through mixed woodland, ignoring a track to the right and continue through a second box gate into a clearing. There are remains of limekilns to the left. Watch out for the healthy population of squirrels. Drop right, into the clearing, and turn left. A blue waymark points to a twisting path ascending opposite you and climbing towards the ridge ahead.

When you breast the ridge you will see a gate ahead of you with a blue waymark – ignore it. Instead, turn sharp left on a good track, passing tall trees, to the ridge. Be wary with children here as you are approaching an open disused quarry. Follow the blue waymark arrows marked 'Ridgeway Path', dipping left to avoid the quarry.

Continue on the clear path to reach Cefn Onn Farm on a minor road. Cross the road and pass to the right of the buildings by stiles, then climb alongside a fence. Stick to the main path, ignoring side tracks, as it heads more or less straight along the ridge. This main path will eventually lead you to the car park opposite the pub. At the car park fence, turn right for a few yards to find a way in.

14 Waterloo, near Machen
The Greenmeadow Inn

Once a port of call for colliers and tinplate workers, the Greenmeadow is still very much a local, though much of the heavy industry is long gone. It is on the hillside above a scattering of houses and well clear of the main road along the Rhymney valley floor. Originally a farmhouse, it became a tavern in the early days of mining. Comfortably furnished, with pictures and brasses on the walls, it is a warm and friendly place. The bar area is large and open plan, with a separate room for a pool table.

The menu is full of good value meals, including T-bone steak, stuffed plaice, lasagne, chicken curry, gammon and steak and kidney pie. Vegetarian dishes, such as curries, are also available. A guest real ale, for example, IPA, joins a range of lagers and cider at the small bar. Sunday dinners are popular here, and booking is essential for them, to avoid disappointment. Afternoon opening hours vary, so a phone call ahead is not a bad idea if you are likely to arrive outside standard lunchtimes.

Telephone: 0633 440323.

How to get there: Waterloo is signposted to the south from the A468 between Bedwas and Machen in the lower Rhymney valley.

46

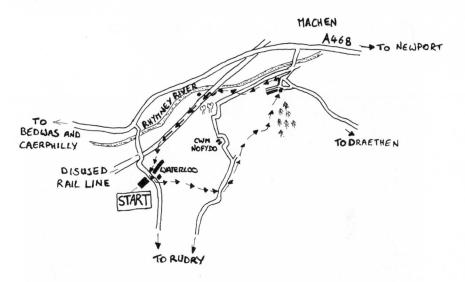

Parking: The pub has a large car park.

Length of the walk: About 3 miles. Map: OS Landranger series 171 Cardiff, Newport and surrounding area (GR 196881).

A fascinating tour through an area once teeming with industry. Iron and coal ruled here once, but no longer. Now the old tramways and rail lines form part of the walk which offers fine views across Machen and the Rhymney valley. The walk is known as the Machen Forge Trail and access to some of it is by permission, not on rights of way.

The Walk

Leave the pub car park and turn right on the road up the hill. Look out for a stile on the left beyond a house, and cross it to a path on the line of an old tramway. Head left through an opening in the fence on the left and across a field. After crossing the next stile, turn right and carry on ascending to a stile which brings you to a mountain road where you turn left.

After about 200 yards look out for the remains of an old tramway bridge. To the right is the site of Pentwyn mine and the tramway used to transport the coal down to the railway. Coal trucks were hoisted and lowered by cable powered by a winding engine. The pit closed in 1930.

Where the road turns left, carry on ahead through a gate and follow the left-hand path until the trees end. Head diagonally right, aiming for a projecting area of woodland enclosed by a low stone wall at the

47

bottom of the field where there is a stile. Cross and turn left into the forestry plantation. The path follows the edge of the plantation down to reach a road.

Go through the gate and turn left down the road. Turn right, pausing to look at Long Row cottages to your left. These were built for workers at Machen Forge in 1871. Go on down the road, turning left before the bridge over the Rhymney. Here you pass Green Row cottages, originally built as a dormitory to house the tough men known as 'sinkers' who prepared mines for working. The lane continues alongside the river to reach a viaduct and disused railway line. The area was the site of Machen Forge, which was in full swing during the Napoleonic Wars, though forges are thought to have operated here since the 16th century. The forge eventually closed in 1886. If you go under the viaduct, some ruins to the left were the stables for the packhorses which carried iron before the tramroad. The main buildings were in Forge Wood, to the left.

Go back under the viaduct and climb steps onto it, turning left to follow it to the end. Go up steps and over a stile into fields. Continue on the path to the left of a hedge to a footbridge. The path leads back to the main road where a left turn leads to the pub.

Ynysddu
The Ynysddu Hotel

The steam engine on the sign swinging outside gives a clue to the past of this freehouse tucked away on the fringe of a small Valleys' village. No trains run along the valley now, but just 40 yards away, hidden among trees, is the site of the old village station. The last passenger train clattered past in 1960 and now the cleared line carries only traffic of a quieter sort – walkers and cyclists. The pub, open from noon until 11 pm Monday to Saturday (with standard Sunday opening times), is a handy and popular port of call.

This an unpretentious place, airy and comfortable, with a separate family room where children are welcome. Outside, benches line a grassy play area with a large treehouse. The owners take food seriously – there is a restaurant upstairs – and although the pub menu offers fairly standard fare, all meals are prepared on the premises, portions are generous and prices modest. They also know how fussy children can be and will do their best to meet special requests. There is a good choice of keg beers, lagers and ciders with a guest real ale, typically Bass, HB or Worthington Best Bitter. It is also a real hotel, offering reasonably priced bed and breakfast accommodation, a convenient overnight halt for walkers tackling the 26-mile Sirhowy Valley Walk which passes nearby.

Telephone: 0495 200281.

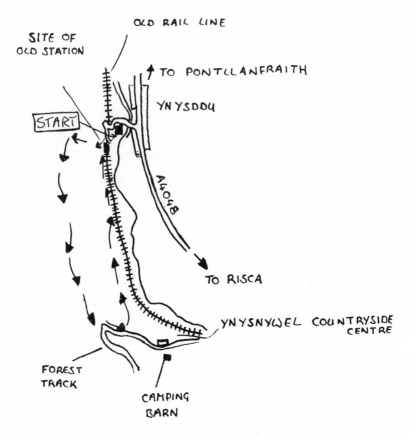

OLD RAIL LINE

SITE OF OLD STATION

TO PONTLLANFRAITH

YNYSDDU

A4048

START

TO RISCA

YNYSNYWEL COUNTRYSIDE CENTRE

FOREST TRACK

CAMPING BARN

How to get there: Ynysddu lies on the A4048 Tredegar road, north-west of Newport. Follow the signposts for the Sirhowy Valley Country Park from the main road in the village (ignoring earlier park signposts if travelling north).

Parking: The entrance to the pub car park is to the left immediately beyond the building and there is also space along the approach road.

Length of the walk: 3 miles. Map: OS Landranger series 171 Cardiff, Newport and surrounding area (GR 177926).

This pleasant walk, quite strenuous at the start, explores the attractive woods on the western hillside of the valley. There are fine views from high above Ynysddu and Cwmfelinfach which give a clear picture of these linear communities, crammed into the valley bottom. It is also a walk with a tale to tell – of an industrial past now greened over and returning to nature. The return leg includes sections along an old tram road which once served a colliery. The route begins and ends on the old railway line, itself originally a tram road built in 1805.

The Walk

From the car park turn left up the lane and take the path on the left on to the old railway line. This is the site of Ynysddu station, though little evidence remains. Cross the line and follow the path uphill into the woods. You are at the start of a long and quite steep haul, soft underfoot in places, and it is better to change into a lower gear and take it steadily than to rush it.

The route has been waymarked with blue flashes but these are patchy in the lower sections. Further on they become more helpful.

Still climbing, go straight on at the first junction. After about 100 yards you meet a small stream. Cross it and continue ascending until the path forks. Take the right-hand path for more upward puffing. Ignore the next right-hand path and go straight on to a stile. Follow the path beyond, turning left and crossing a small stream. As the track levels out, you pass ruins to your left and extensive views open out across the valley. Immediately past the ruins, take the right-hand path through lovely ancient beech woods. A bench seat at the pathside offers a welcome chance to catch your breath and enjoy the view.

Shortly after the seat, cross a stile and follow a forest path with Scots pine on the left and Japanese larch on the right. You presently emerge on to a Forestry Commission road, lined with birch and rowan, which is the highest point of the walk. Turn left down this road and the good surface allows you to stride out. At a prominent television mast turn left and continue along the road to a hairpin bend.

At this point a detour down the road which turns sharply right will take you to the Ynyshywel Farm countryside centre.

Our route carries straight on at the hairpin, descending into the woods. You soon reach another track, which used to be the tram road leading to Wentloog colliery, now disused.

Near the end of the track, shattered red brick underfoot and remnants of buildings among the trees are all that remain of Ynysddu Brickworks, which supplied the material for many of the houses in Ynysddu. Turn left on to the old railway line and walk back to the starting point. As you walk reflect on the fact that the first steam locomotive on the line was the Britannia, modelled on Stephenson's famous Rocket, which started service here in 1829. How times have changed!

16 Cosmeston
The Schooner

The name of this pub is a little misleading, unless it refers to the children's play boat outside! In fact the grey stone building was, until a quarter of a century ago, offices for cement works connected to nearby quarries which have been beautifully reclaimed as Cosmeston Lakes Country Park.

There is no trace of the dust of industry now, and the spacious interior is very comfortably furnished. Plenty of plush seating surrounds tables in the bar area and in the separate restaurant section. The carvery is well worth checking out. It offers a choice of hot roast joints, carved to order, self-serve vegetables and trimmings, all good value, with half-price portions for children. There is a good choice of bar meals, too, with a daily range of specials like turkey and mushroom pie. Keep an eye out for the monthly specials – the 20 oz rump steak with trimmings takes some beating (and eating). All the food is prepared and cooked on the premises. As you would expect at a Bass Tavern, draught Bass is available, along with the popular Hancock's HB real ale. The wine of the week promotions might, however, tempt you away from the beer. One point to note, the Schooner is open all day Sunday for food (and accompanying drinks) from 12 noon to 10 pm.

Telephone: 0222 704200.

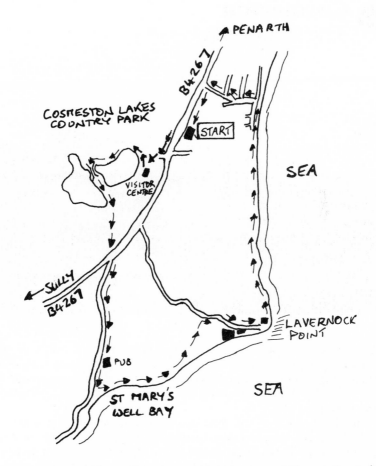

How to get there: The pub is close to the signposted Cosmeston Lakes Country Park on the B4267 road between Penarth and Barry.

Parking: There is a large car park adjoining the pub.

Length of the walk: About 3½ miles. Map: OS Landranger series 171 Cardiff, Newport and surrounding area (GR 181693).

A lakeside stroll, sea views, a chance for some beachcombing, and a spot of history are on the menu for this gentle, easy walk. Attached to the country park near the start is a fascinating experiment in recreating a medieval village − opening times are limited but there is a colourful display in the visitor centre and the thatched buildings can be clearly seen along the way.

The Walk

From the pub car park walk left down the main road. Cross, with care, to turn right into the entrance of Cosmeston Lakes Country Park. Walk to the right of the visitor centre and turn right along the perimeter of the lake on a good path, pausing, perhaps, to feed the ducks and swans. Go right around the lake, passing an enticing adventure playground to the right, until you reach a path junction. Turn left, crossing a bridge, and continue straight ahead on the broad track. The medieval village can be seen across fields to the left before you reach the main road.

Cross the road and go down the lane directly opposite, signposted 'St Mary's Well Bay'. Pass the Golden Hind pub on the left and, just beyond a gateway, turn left on to a footpath. You will shortly reach a steep concrete pathway to the beach. If the tide is right (low or ebbing), you may turn left and walk along the mainly pebble and stone-terraced beach, all the way to Lavernock Point, the site of Marconi's first radio transmission across water, in 1897. Regain the cliff path by steps a short distance beyond the point. Even if the tide prevents that option, you can explore the small, pebbly bay, climbing out by rock steps at the far end.

If in any doubt about the tide, though, continue on the cliff path, with the caravan park on your left. Take care, of course, to keep children away from the cliff edges which are crumbling in places. Pass to the right of a pillbox and continue, glimpsing old military installations on both sides, and later chalets belonging to the Marconi Country Club on your right. Go through a metal kissing-gate and turn right along a minor road. Pass the church (note the inscription commemorating Marconi's historic broadcast) and a derelict farm, then turn left into a clear path through bushes.

Beyond Lavernock Point, stride out along a good stretch of path atop low cliffs, with views to Penarth ahead. There are a number of pleasant grassy places to pause and a chance to pop safely down on to the beach if the fancy takes you – though take care.

As you enter the outskirts of Penarth, the path becomes a wide, grassy promenade. Keep an eye out to your left for Stanton Way, the first proper road running away from the front, and turn up it. Follow the road around the first right turn, and then go left, crossing an old railway line. Go straight on, passing a grocery store, to reach the main road. Turn left to regain the pub car park.

17 Caerphilly Mountain
The Traveller's Rest

Caerphilly 'mountain' may be only 888 ft high but the views can be spectacular. The Traveller's Rest, high on the hill, makes an ideal base from which to explore the bracken and fern-covered slopes of Caerphilly Common and the wooded Wennalt.

Six-footers should beware as they step into the bar of this thatched former coaching inn, the low, beamed ceilings having caused quite a few sore heads. The small bar, with an open fire in an impressive fireplace in winter, is always cosy and wooden settles, flagstones and exposed stone walls are in keeping with the building's 350 year history. Families will find room to spread themselves in the unexpectedly large lounge to the left. In fine weather the extensive beer garden with benches is, of course, a popular option. The pub is a favourite stopping place for walkers and for family outings and its ploughman's lunch, with a choice of cheeses, pâté or peppered mackerel, is famous in the area. There are open sandwiches too and the menu offers a good range of meals, for example, lasagne, chicken tikka masala and beef and venison pie, with vegetarian options. Real ales include Bass, Hancock's HB and guest beers like Wadworth 6X.

Telephone: 0222 886894.

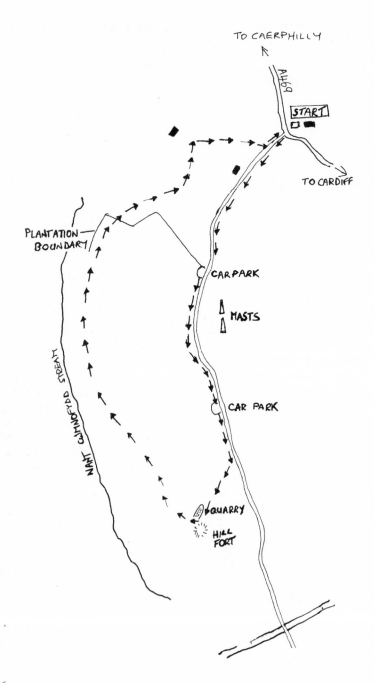

TO CAERPHILLY

A469

START

TO CARDIFF

PLANTATION
BOUNDARY

CAR PARK

MASTS

NANT CWMNOFYDD STREAM

CAR PARK

QUARRY

HILL
FORT

How to get there: The inn is on the A469 mountain road between Cardiff and Caerphilly, 2 miles south of Caerphilly on the Cardiff side.

Parking: The pub has a large car park. There is also a car park nearby in the Caerphilly direction, serving the common.

Length of the walk: 2½ miles. Map: OS Landranger series 171 Cardiff, Newport and surrounding area (GR 158844).

A delightful route at any time of year, though the bluebell display in early summer is particularly lovely. It is largely through attractive woodland, owned by the city of Cardiff, with fine views from the top end. The walk can easily be combined with a visit to Caerphilly Castle, the second largest in Europe after Windsor Castle.

The Walk

With your back to the pub car park, cross the road carefully, and go down the lane opposite (Wenalt Road), passing Witts End cottage. Continue down the quiet lane and as you approach radio masts on the left, you will see a car park off the lane to the right.

From the car park follow a path under Scots pines, running more or less alongside the lane. You soon come to a second car park in front of a large open grassy area. Cross to the far edge of this field and bear right to take the clear path ascending gently into trees – ignore another track descending left.

There is something of a maze of small tracks around here, but the main path is not difficult to follow. Pass a memorial seat and then a deep cleft, the remains of a quarry, to your right. The surrounding banks and bumps are spoil heaps. A poorly defined hill fort lies ahead now. The path descends, swinging round to the right beneath mature deciduous trees. At a fork bear left, going down to a clear path running along the fringe of the woods up a small valley.

Continue along this good path to an old stone wall. A right turn before this wall climbs back to emerge on the road near the first car park. Instead, cross the stile and climb right, diagonally across a field, to a stile in the top corner. Walk ahead towards a small wood, where there is a waymark on a post. Go through the copse, with a paddock fence above you to the right, and cross a small fence. Ahead to the left you will see a large white house. Keep to the path between this house and a farm with outbuildings above you. As you pass by the farm above, bear right, diagonally upwards, to a small fenced enclosure beside a drive. A stile at the right-hand end of this enclosure, and another opposite, brings you to the lane you started on. Turn left and retrace your steps to the main road. Cross carefully back to the pub.

⑱ Cardiff (Llandaff)
The Black Lion

The black timber-frame and whitewashed walls of the Black Lion make it look more like a village inn than a street-corner city pub. But then Llandaff, like other Cardiff suburbs, retains a village atmosphere.

Although it is at the junction of a main road and side street, the pub is just 200 yards or so from the entrance to Llandaff Cathedral and its attractive surroundings – it is hard to believe you are in a capital city. One reminder is the fact that it is a Brains house – the Cardiff brewery which still produces real ale right in the heart of the city centre. The full range of highly regarded Brains beers is on offer here, Bitter, the stronger SA and Dark – a mild. There is also a choice of 20 malt whiskies, plus lagers, Guinness and cider at the bar.

This is a typically comfortable, no-frills pub with a large, open lounge where children are welcome for meals. Food is plentiful and reasonably priced. Examples from the menu include curries, steak and kidney pie and lasagne. Cod, peas and chips and tuna salad are lighter options, with a good range of toasted sandwiches.

Telephone: ex-directory.

58

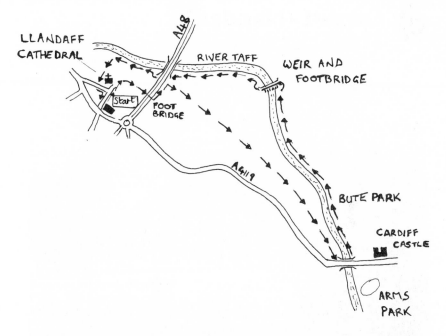

How to get there: The pub is near Llandaff Cathedral in a north-western Cardiff suburb. The easiest approach is by the A48, Western Avenue. Follow signs to Llandaff and the cathedral. The Black Lion is on the corner of Cardiff Road and High Street.

Parking: There is no pub car park, but some roadside parking is available in side streets. It is, perhaps, easier to park near the cathedral and walk the short distance back.

Length of the walk: About 4½ miles. Maps: OS Landranger series 171 Cardiff, Newport and surrounding area, or OS Pathfinder series 1165 Cardiff and Penarth (GR 155778).

An easy, pleasant walk through the Welsh capital's lovely parks. The route connects two of the city's best-known historic sites − Cardiff Castle and Llandaff Cathedral − and offers a view of another famous place of worship − Cardiff Arms Park.

The Walk

With your back to the pub at the street corner, turn right up High Street towards the cathedral. Carry straight on down Cathedral Close, passing St Teilo's Well on your left. This is reputedly the site of a well associated with St Teilo, consecrated as the second Bishop of Llandaff in the 6th century. The lane passes to the right of the cathedral and swings right, alongside the graveyard, to become a path flanked by fencing.

You soon emerge on a main road (Western Avenue) with the Llandaff Rugby Club on the left. Turn left to cross a footbridge over the road, and continue left on the far side. After about 50 yards turn right at a cycle way/footpath sign onto a broad, surfaced park road. This avenue, sometimes flanked by tall trees, runs virtually straight through Pontcanna fields. You pass the City of Cardiff Riding School to the left and a playground off to the right, then a municipal caravan site. There are playing fields everywhere and there is usually something happening on a weekend afternoon – I paused to watch an American football match.

The avenue continues past Glamorgan County Cricket Ground, the Welsh National Sports Centre and Sophia Gardens to reach the end of the park beside a bridge over the Taff. Leave the park by a riverside exit to your left, and cross the Taff. To your right you can see the National Stadium (widely known as the Arms Park), the home of Welsh rugby.

To visit Cardiff Castle, carry straight on to reach the entrance on the left.

Otherwise, turn left just beyond the bridge, through impressive wooden gates, to enter Bute Park Arboretum. From here, stick to the surfaced track nearest the river, passing a stone circle and, later, a sundial sculpture. You pass greenhouses enclosed by a high wall, and, as you reach the end of the wall, go left from the surfaced track as it swings rightwards, to take a path beside the river. This wends its frequently muddy way through brush and shrubbery, often close to the water.

After an impressive weir, cross the footbridge and turn right to follow a path close to the river on the far side. The path exits onto a road beside a bridge. This is a busy road (Western Avenue, crossed earlier by footbridge), so go left for a few yards until you can use an island to cross more safely. On the other side of the road, go through an entrance to reach a riverside embankment path. Continue on this path until you pass the line of the cathedral steeple, away to the left. Around here, a wooden post marks a path dropping off left to a metal gate. Cross a small field towards the cathedral, to another gate. Beyond this, carry straight on up a steep lane, which goes past the front of the cathedral, to emerge above it near a large cross. Bear left, then right, to reach High Street and the Black Lion.

Taff's Well
The Taff's Well Inn

19

The pub and village are named after a spring beside the river Taff with reputed healing powers, now sadly closed to visitors. Such was its renown that the area was known as the Valley of the Sticks, because disabled visitors were said to throw them away after taking the waters.

No such claims are made by this Ansells pub, though a reviving drink will probably be welcome after the walk. The Taff's Well Inn was originally a farm and its history has been traced to 1750, the century it became a coaching house. Nowadays the beamed ceiling has been enclosed, but the wood panelling and rustic style make it a comfortable and welcoming place. It is a friendly, 'no frills' pub, serving home-made, good-value meals in generous portions. Main courses like liver and bacon and roast chicken are supplemented by specials, which include pasta Italienne, curries and chilli. Children's meals like fish fingers, chips and a Coke for an all-in price are a boon for families. Tetley Bitter is the regular real ale, joined by a guest beer, such as Walker Best, which changes every fortnight.

Telephone: 0222 813476.

How to get there: The pub is on the A4054 in the village of Taff's Well, north-west of Cardiff. It is easily reached via the A470 Pontypridd road.

61

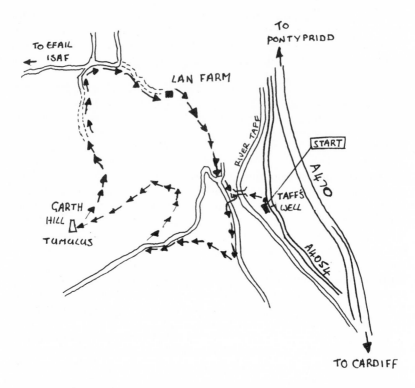

Parking: There is limited parking beside the pub and roadside parking elsewhere.

Length of the walk: About 4 miles. Map: OS Landranger series 171 Cardiff, Newport and surrounding area (GR 120837).

An excellent, energetic circuit involving a long, sustained climb from the riverside to the top of Garth Hill. The magnificent views and fresh breezes are worth every step.

The Walk

With your back to the pub, turn left and, a few yards along, turn left again in front of a school, into a lane. Follow the lane to the right (yellow arrow) and cross the footbridge over the Taff.

Go through a subway, not much improved by murals, and climb a steep, switch-back path lined with railings. Take it steadily as there is plenty of climbing still to come. At the road turn left, descending past a school to your left. Ignore a footpath signpost pointing to the right between fences. Soon after, another footpath is signposted to the right, climbing diagonally from the road into the trees. Take this broad track and as it bends right, go through a wooden gate and continue climbing. Stick to this main track, climbing steeply, ignoring junctions.

You soon reach the top edge of the woods, bearing slightly left to reach and go through a wooden gate into a pasture. Head for a metal kissing-gate, directly opposite, which leads on to a minor road. Turn left and walk along the road for a few minutes, passing a picnic area path on the right and an old farmhouse on the left.

Soon after the farm building take a path on the right which climbs the hillside, almost doubling back on the road. Climb steadily, using stone steps in places and crossing a small stream. You soon reach a rocky outcrop – a fine viewpoint and a convenient spot for a breather. See if you can spot your car parked far below in the valley.

From the outcrop, climb the path which rises steeply behind it, with the steep hillside to your right. As you crest the first bump look to your left and you should see the tumulus summit mound of Garth Hill, topped by a triangulation pillar, on the skyline. Follow a clear path veering rightwards to it. Views to the Brecon Beacons to the north, and across the Bristol Channel to the south are well worth all that huffing and puffing.

At the tumulus turn to face the direction from which you have just come. Take a track to the left of, and initially almost parallel to, the path you used in the approach. This soon turns sharply leftwards and descends the northern flank of the hill.

Hop over a stile and the track becomes a sunken lane. A couple more stiles and you pass derelict farm buildings. Just below the buildings turn right downhill on a metalled road through a gate, over a stile and another gate. At a junction with a minor road, follow it rightwards, ignoring a left turn a few yards further on.

At a sharp turn in the road turn right through a gated entrance (marked Lan Farm) on to a track. Follow this track, after a little while passing through the farm buildings (weaving right, left, right and left again through the barns). Just beyond, a wooden gate leads to a forest track on the top edge of the woods. Descend quite steeply, keeping right when a good track tempts you left. Soon go through a metal gate and emerge on the road at a hairpin bend. Turn left and when you reach the Gwaelod y Garth Inn, turn right on to the road, and keep an eye out for the path with railings you climbed at the start of the walk. Retrace your steps to the Taff's Well Inn.

⓴ **Pentwyn, near Fochriw**
The White Horse Inn

Non-Welsh speakers take note, 'Tafarn Ceffil Gwyn' means White Horse Inn. The Welsh name is what you see as you approach from either direction, but it is in English on the front for a double check.

This freehouse, high up the Darran valley in the hamlet of Pentwyn, is a traditional pub, more than 100 years old, with Coronation mugs, mining pictures and lamps on the walls. An old blacklead grate and hob is an interesting feature. Cow Pie stands out on the menu – Desperate Dan's favourite meal is served here without the horns but with beef, carrots and onions and is a popular choice. The landlady prepares her own ham and it is served with salad or potatoes. Other options include standards like chicken, fish and gammon, all very reasonably priced. Hancock's HB is the real ale on offer, with keg bitters, Guinness, Tennent's Extra and Carling Black Label. Casual trade must be limited in this remote spot but the pub is deservedly popular and can get very busy. If you want to eat here, it is wise to ring first to check opening times and, in holiday times, to make sure you can be fitted in.

Telephone: 0685 841215.

How to get there: The White Horse is 2 miles north of Deri and just south of Fochriw on a minor road connecting Bargoed in the Rhymney valley with Merthyr Tydfil. This minor road runs parallel with the A469.

Parking: The pub has a small car park and the roadside parking nearby is plentiful.

Length of the walk: About 5 miles. Map: OS Landranger series 171 Cardiff, Newport and surrounding area (GR 105045).

A varied and scenic circuit in a former mining area, now beautifully reclaimed and developed as a country park.

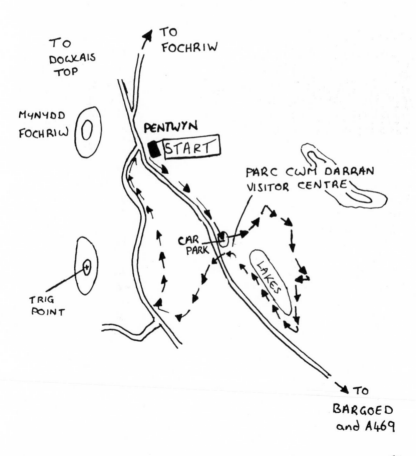

The Walk

With your back to the pub, turn left down the road. Continue down the hill, bearing left and passing the old Deri school building on your left. At a signpost for Cwm Darran picnic site and viewpoint, turn left into the car park and then head left for the signposted path to the visitor centre.

Follow the footpath down until it meets a ballasted track and turn left – do not go right to the visitor centre. The track bears right and approaches a river. About 20 yards before the river turn left to follow a path across a footbridge to a stile. Cross over and follow the path up through forestry.

The path steepens and curves to the left before joining a grassy track. Turn right, back on yourself, and follow the track for some 80 yards until you see a steep track leading up to the left. Follow this through forestry to a clearing under power cables with the ruins of Brithdir Uchaf Farm. A firebreak in the trees gives a good view of Cwm Darran campsite.

Continue with the ruin on your left and forestry on the right, go through a gate and emerge from the trees. Follow the track around to the right and almost back on yourself. The track heads straight down and as you go enjoy the views up the valley with the White Horse on the horizon.

The track swings sharply left and Deri lakes and the Darran valley can now be seen. Follow the track to the bottom and cross a stile. Turn right and head towards the lakes. Turn left through a little car park and head for a footbridge across a small weir. Follow the path to the right and walk along the lakeside.

At the top end of the lake the path joins a track, which is followed, passing an adventure playground on your left. Pass the visitor centre, also on your left, and continue on the road up and to the left to reach the main road. Turn right up the road for about 100 yards. Ignore a bridleway sign on your left, but take the next path on the left, which leads to a stile. Cross and follow the footpath heading straight up, going through old gates. Head for a gate in the corner of the field, turn right and go through two gates. Take the lower path and follow it to the right. Continue for about ¾ mile, parallel with a dry-stone wall.

You will now see the Mount Pleasant Inn. At the pub, turn right to reach the main road, from where you will see the White Horse. Turn right over the cattle grid and walk down to the pub.

21 Llancarfan
The Fox and Hounds

The writhing spaghetti of lanes and back roads and rolling farmland
of the Vale of Glamorgan could hardly be a greater contrast to the
valleys to the north. Llancarfan is one of dozens of small, peaceful
hamlets alongside roads going nowhere in particular.

Dating back to the 16th century, the Fox and Hounds riverside
village inn wins top marks for both beer and food. Its regular beers –
Brains, Ruddles and John Smith's – are joined by two or three guest
ales like Hardington Moonshine and Fuller's ESB. Hungry walkers will
find it difficult to choose between the good value bar meals and eating
in the separate restaurant upstairs. In the bar, Huntsman's Pie – steak
and kidney in a rich, dark sauce – and Vegetable Mexicana – broccoli
and cauliflower in a spicy sauce with cheese topping – are just two
of the very reasonably priced examples. For sheer value, though, the
lunch of three courses plus coffee takes some beating. There is also a
separate children's menu which includes vegieburgers, and a number
of bar meals are available in lower-priced children's portions. In the
restaurant, a four-course Sunday lunch is served each week, with main
courses like roast leg of Welsh lamb or pork chop in red wine sauce.
The inn's honeycomb of rooms are kept cosy with coal fires in winter,

and in summer the patio running down to the river is used for weekend barbecues.
Telephone: 0446 781297.

How to get there: The pub is in the village of Llancarfan, south-west of Cardiff. It is about 3 miles from the A48 at Bonvilston, where the village exit is signposted.

Parking: There is plenty of parking beside the pub, with additional space across the stream via a bridge.

Length of the walk: About 5 miles. Map: OS Landranger series 170 Vale of Glamorgan and Rhondda area (GR 050703).

A varied walk, taking in open farmland, woods and hedge-lined lanes in this attractive rural backwater,where you are more than likely to have the paths to yourselves.

The Walk

With your back to the stream at the rear of the pub, turn right and follow the road north out of the village – it is the road you are most likely to have come in on. Go past two fords over the stream to your right. Shortly after the second you will see a footpath signpost beside a gate – ignore it. Instead, take a grassy lane trending off to the left just beyond it, to the left of a large stone house. Go through a gate into a field and cross it, keeping a stream to your right. Go through another gate and cross a small field to a wooden stile and small footbridge. Cross the field beyond, bearing rightwards. Aim for a white farmhouse on the skyline ahead of you.

As you approach the farm, head towards outbuildings to the right of the house. Go through double gates just to the left of the outbuildings and cross a stableyard, exiting via a gate ahead of you on to a concrete drive. Follow the drive across open fields to a minor road. Go through a gate directly opposite (yellow waymark arrow) and head on towards a wood, with a hedge to your right. At the end of the field, go right through a small wooden gate and turn left to follow the field perimeter.

Stay close to the boundary of the woods to your left and when you reach a rough track, follow it leftwards down into the trees. Go through a gate, and the track soon emerges into a field. Aim for a pylon ahead and to the left (the nearest of a line of pylons), reached via an open gateway. Go to the right of the pylon and descend towards a hamlet with the hedge on your right. At the bottom of the field, climb a rickety stile, then a good mini-bridge, and cross the next field to a

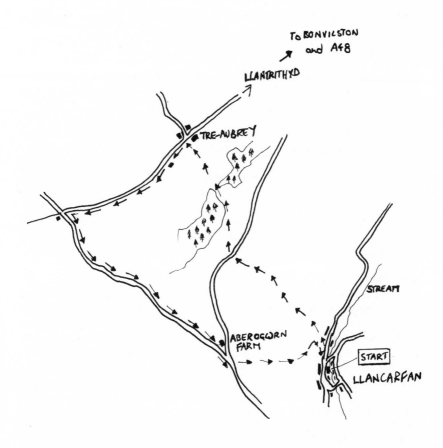

stile which brings you to a minor road at Tre-Aubrey.

Turn left along the minor road, passing Wren's Castle Farm on your left. Continue until a crossroads and turn left, signposted 'Llancadle'. The road passes between the scattered farms which form Treguff and crosses a small footbridge before rising, quite sharply for a while, to a road junction by Aberogwrn Farm.

Immediately beyond the junction, cross a tall stile to the left into a large field and walk straight ahead, with the hedge to your left. Continue beside the hedge, eventually crossing a stile. As the hedge swings leftwards, leave it, descending towards the left edge of a wood, with Llancarfan village beyond. A stile just to the left of the woods leads into a steeply sloping field. Descend to the left of the nearest building and go through a gate to a road. Turn right to return to the pub.

22 St Hilary
The Bush Inn

A thatched pub next to the church, horse-riders clopping past – a scene so typically English you have to pinch yourself to remember this is Wales. Tucked away in the centre of a pretty Vale of Glamorgan village, this is the sort of inn Hollywood film-makers think we all have on our doorsteps.

The Bush, which dates back hundreds of years, continues the traditional theme inside, with low-beamed ceilings, high wooden settles and cosy bars. Laverbread (seaweed) on the menu, though, confirms its Welshness. Indeed, Welsh dishes are a speciality, mingling with French cuisine on the à la carte menu of the pub's attractive restaurant. Faggots and peas may be on offer in the bar along with steak and ale pie and staples like not-so-Welsh curry and lasagne. Customers in pursuit of a traditional hangover may like to sample the real scrumpy – a wiser bet might be real ale, with a choice from Reverend James, Bass and Old Speckled Hen.

If you want even more proof that the pub has something going for it, consider this. The thatched roof has suffered a number of fires over the years. While firemen tackled one of them, not so long ago, regulars kept track of the action from where they like it best – in the bar, drinking. Well, that is the tale the landlord tells.

Telephone: 0446 772745.

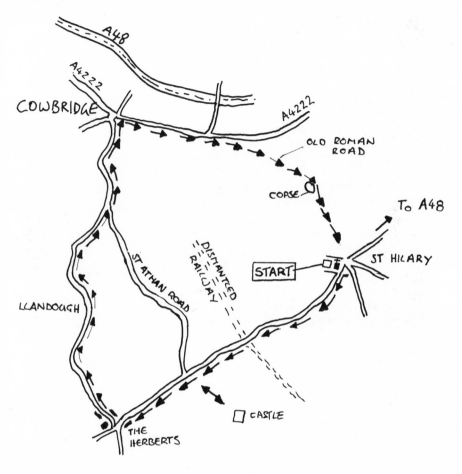

How to get there: The pub is beside the church in the village of St Hilary, just south of the A48 and east of Cowbridge.

Parking: Around the pub. There is also limited roadside parking in the village.

Length of the walk: About 5 miles. Maps: OS Landranger series 170 Vale of Glamorgan and Rhondda area (GR 016734).

An enjoyable and easy circuit, mainly on quiet country lanes, through typical Vale of Glamorgan rural scenery, with the option of a visit to the atmospheric ruins of Beaupre Castle. The walk also includes a stretch along a well-preserved Roman road. Keep an eye out for buzzards and squirrels.

The Walk

With your back to the Bush, turn left and then right, around the front of the church, taking the narrow road out of the village. At a road junction turn right, signposted 'St Mary Church' and descend the quiet country lane between hedgerows. Cross a disused railway line, and turn left at a junction, to a bridge.

A footpath from the bridge leads left across meadows to the impressive ruins of Beaupre Castle.

The road then ascends to a junction at The Herberts. Turn right, signposted 'Llandough', passing a tiny and unexpected car showroom on your left. After a couple of switchbacks the road crosses a stream and then climbs to a junction. Turn right and follow the road, which dips to cross a steam before climbing out of the far side of a little valley.

At a junction with a main road opposite a farm, turn left and follow the road which soon trends right, climbing into the outskirts of Cowbridge. Take care on this short stretch as it is the only busy section of the whole route. The road leads to a junction with traffic lights on the main road through Cowbridge.

Turn right at the lights, up a hill (Cardiff Road/Primrose Hill). Ignore footpath signs and continue for about ½ mile until a broad track, a Roman road, can be seen diverging right from the road near a bus stop. Follow the track, climbing steadily, to the transmitter masts and distinctive copse at the top of Stalling Down. Head clockwise around the trees and turn to the right, down a clear track, aiming for the church tower in St Hilary. At the road junction turn right and return to the pub.

Monknash
(23) The Plough and Harrow

If you like a pub with a past, this is the place for you. Around 600 years old, the low, stone building was originally part of a monastery, the ruins of which are scattered around the little community. The Plough and Harrow is on the edge of the village, with nothing but fields between it and the Bristol Channel. It has been a pub for 500 years and the place oozes character with oak beams, flagstone floors, wooden benches and, in winter, a big open fire in the bar. Outside is surely one of the quietest beer gardens around – tables surrounded by stone walls with open fields beyond. A section of the bar is believed to have been used as a mortuary at one time – does this mean you can enjoy beer with body?

Beer is the speciality, with regulars Worthington Best, Flowers Original, Hancock's HB and Marston's Pedigree joined by guest ales. Traditional country food is the aim of the menu, all home-cooked and at modest prices. Meals may be available only at lunchtime – telephone for details.

Telephone: 065 679 209.

How to get there: The pub is signposted in the village of Monknash, on a minor road off the B4265, south of Wick, and about 8 miles south of Bridgend.

73

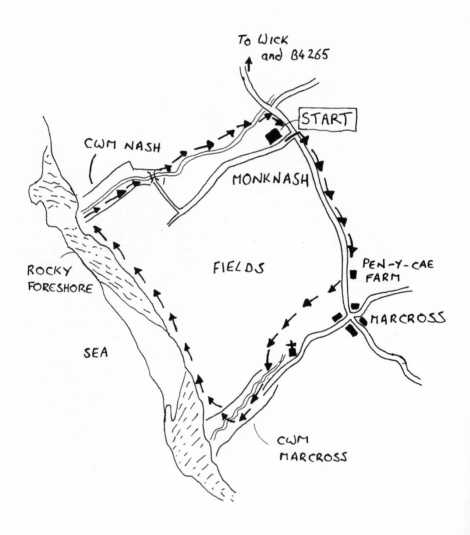

To WICK
and B4265

START

CWM NASH

MONKNASH

ROCKY
FORESHORE

FIELDS

PEN-Y-CAE
FARM

MARCROSS

SEA

CWM
MARCROSS

Parking: There is a car park almost opposite the pub. Plent͵
alternative parking is available on verges in and around the village.

Length of the walk: About 4 miles. Map: OS Landranger series 170 Vale
of Glamorgan and Rhondda area (GR 919706).

*The walking is easy and there is much to enjoy on this pleasant circuit which takes
in a nature reserve, a lengthy clifftop section and passes close to the atmospheric
remains of a monastery.*

The Walk

With your back to the pub, turn left to reach a road junction and turn
right, signposted to St Donats. Continue along the road, passing farm
buildings on the right and left until you reach Pen-y-cae Farm (name
on gate) on your left. A few yards beyond the farm, cross a stone stile
on your right, into a field, and walk ahead beside the hedge. Keep an
eye out for a stile to your right and cross over into another field.
Continue in the same direction as before, with the hedge to your left.

Cross another stile, pass to the right of a house, and a stile on your
left leads you towards a wood. Cross a marshy stream bed, skirting the
wood, to enter a wooded gully, a nature reserve. There are two paths
though the reserve – take your pick – both bring you to the same
spot at the far end.

On leaving the woods, turn right on a broad, grassy path climbing
easily and quickly to the clifftop. Take care with children at this point.
Cross a stone stile into a field and carry on, safely inside a fence, with
the cliff edge on your left. Continue, crossing a number of stiles, until
the path descends to a small bay. Keep close to the fence to find the
easiest way down. Turn to the right in front of a wall, and follow a
clear path over a stile and into the woods. Soon see houses on the
other side of the stream, and the path emerges on a road.

Ignore a footpath sign almost opposite. Instead turn left towards a
little bridge and set of driveway gates. Use stiles on both sides of the
gate to get around it, cross the drive, and to the right of the gate
another stile brings you into a field.

From here the path heads back to Monknash, to the left of a stream,
crossing several fields. Keep the stream to your right and you cannot
miss the succession of stiles. Eventually you will come to a wall
blocking the way, with ruined monastery buildings beyond. Drop to
the right to cross the stream by stepping stones and turn left over a
stile. Go straight ahead, passing the monastery ruins, and aim for two
outbuildings with a gate between them. To their left a stile gives access
to a road. Turn right and walk back towards the village and the
junction near the pub.

24 **Pontneddfechan**
The Angel

Its closeness to the beautiful gorges and waterfalls which lie immediately behind has meant the Angel has featured in travel literature for many years. Cliff's 1848 *Book of South Wales* told visitors 'A guide may be hired from the primitive hostelrie of the Angel', when it was nothing more than a squalid little room. Scientist Michael Faraday, then assistant to Sir Humphry Davy of miner's lamp fame, stayed in the attic of the original building and wrote about the waterfall country. The old part of the pub, which still offers accommodation, was originally Angel Farm and the tourist information centre opposite is on the site of its barn. Nowadays the pub has been well modernised, split into a large, comfortable lounge and smaller, tile-floored Hikers' Bar for muddy boot customers. A small cobbled area at the front of the pub has tables and benches.

Food is plentiful and good value. Starters include breaded mushrooms with garlic mayonnaise and there are main meals like home-made steak and kidney pie, broccoli and cream cheese bake, and lamb chops. Bass is on draught plus a guest real ale, such as Boddingtons, and the usual range of cider and lagers.

Telephone: 0639 722013.

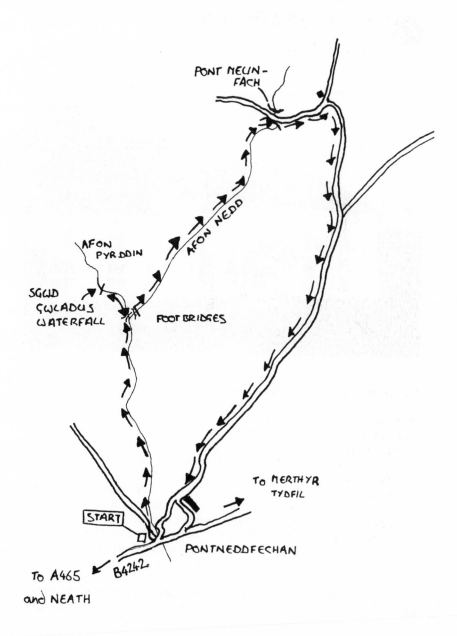

PONT MELIN-FACH

AFON PYRDDIN

AFON NEDD

SGWD GWLADUS WATERFALL

FOOTBRIDGES

TO MERTHYR TYDFIL

START

PONTNEDDFECHAN

TO A465 and NEATH

B4242

How to get there: The Angel is about 1 mile north-east of Glyn-neath at the end of the B4242, reached via Neath and the A465.

Parking: In the pub car park and on the roadside nearby.

Length of the walk: About 5 miles. Map: OS Landranger series 160 Brecon Beacons (GR 901076).

A marvellous exploration of scenic gorges and waterfalls, rewarding in any weather and at any time of year. The walk rises high above the river and offers spectacular scenery – take care with your footing and keep an eye on young children as you go. The route can be made circular by returning on quiet minor roads or you may prefer to retrace your steps for a different perspective.

The Walk

Immediately behind the pub go through the iron gate and walk upstream with the river on your right. The path is clear throughout and route-finding is easy. Look out for cascades above you on the sides of the gorge. At the meeting of the Afon Nedd and a tributary, the Afon Pyrddin, there is a footbridge which you will cross – but not yet. Instead, turn left and follow a path with the tributary on your right to a viewing platform for the magical Sgwd Gwladus waterfall.

Retrace your steps and cross the footbridge. Continue upstream with the Nedd on your right, ignoring another footbridge over the river. The path rises and falls, steeply in places, passing a succession of cascades. Some are far below, others close, notably the Upper Ddwli Falls – a great place for a rest or picnic.

As you cross a bouncy footbridge spare a thought for those who built it – the gorge is so inaccessible it was airlifted in. Continue through beautiful woodland until eventually the path opens out into a large clearing with picnic benches at Pont Melin-fach, the site of an old mill and limekilns, where there is an information board.

Here you have a choice – go back the way you have come, or take to country lanes. If you prefer the latter, cross the bridge by the picnic area and climb right up the narrow road. Keep bearing right along the road, ignoring turnings to the left, to return to the village.

If you choose to retrace your steps, take the opportunity for a closer look at Sgwd Gwladus. At the junction of the rivers turn right before crossing the footbridge. The path leads to the falls and it is possible to clamber up and view the rim. Return, cross the footbridge to the far bank and continue back to the pub.

25 Ogmore
The Pelican Inn

Overlooking peaceful watermeadows and almost opposite the lane leading to Ogmore Castle in the straggling hamlet of the same name, this is a well-known venue for real ale enthusiasts. It has been a pub since well into the last century and takes its name from an element in the coat of arms of a prominent local family. There is plenty of wood everywhere in this comfortable inn, with high, timber ceilings and rustic framing. A huge, double fireplace and chimney divides the bar – an attractive feature – and there is a separate lounge where children are welcome. Benches on a terrace with a play frame offer a good view of the castle.

Fresh fish is the pub's speciality with cod and plaice always on the menu and such variations as plaice stuffed with prawns and mushrooms. Wherever possible, everything is home-made, like the steak and ale pie and the quiche. Sunday lunch offers starters like garlic mushrooms and desserts such as apple pie, with the main course a choice from three roast meats. There is a good selection of real ales, for example, Brains SA and Dark, Courage Best, Old Speckled Hen, Wadworth 6X and John Smith's Yorkshire Bitter. For non-beer drinkers there are up to three draught ciders among the many taps lining the timbered bar.

Telephone: 0656 880049.

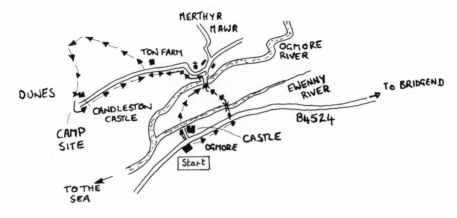

How to get there: The pub is beside the B4524 in Ogmore (not nearby Ogmore-by-Sea). The nearest M4 junction is 35.

Parking: The pub has a large car park.

Length of the walk: About 3½ miles. Map: OS Landranger series 170 Vale of Glamorgan and Rhondda area (GR 882767).

A lovely walk, packing a lot of variety in a modest distance – a castle, a river crossing, springy pasture and dunes – and the possibility of extending it to the beach.

The Walk

Take the lane almost opposite the pub, signposted to the castle, which is worth a once-over. Just beyond the castle lies the Ewenny river and decision time. If the stepping stones are exposed (and you feel up to it) cross over and then follow the path, swinging rightwards across meadows to reach the mini-suspension bridge over the more substantial Ogmore river.

If the stepping stones are not feasible, retrace your steps to the road and turn left along the grass verge (or pavement opposite). After about 400 yards, go through a metal gate beside a bus shelter, follow the path across a footbridge and head diagonally leftwards across the field to reach the same suspension bridge.

Beyond the bridge follow the road ahead and you quickly reach the tiny green in the centre of Merthyr Mawr, with a lovely thatched house ahead. Take the left fork in the road and continue left. The quiet lane passes a church on the right, and then swings right. Carry on to Ton Fruit Farm, also the office for Candleston campsite, which you pass later. Just beyond the farm cross a stone stile on the right and walk straight on, climbing steadily with a fence to the right.

At the top right corner of the field, a junction of two high walls, cross a stone stile and continue ahead with a fence on your right. Diverge left from the fence and as you crest the brow of the rise you will see a clear, grassy trail descending quite steeply to the bottom of a small valley with woods beyond. Follow it down, heading for a gate ahead in the wall running the length of the valley. Cross the small stream before the wall and look for a stone stile about 20 yards to the left of the gate. Cross and turn left to the end of the wall. Follow the signposted footpath for 'Candleston Castle'. It is a clear track ahead with pines on the left. The track is liable to flooding after heavy rain and you may have to dodge from side to side for a short while, but it soon becomes dry.

The ruins of Candleston Castle are passed to the left and the track swings round to a car park. Here you have the chance to cross the dunes for a mile to the beach.

Otherwise, bear left through the car park and take the lane – the campsite entrance is to the right. Continue along the lane to return to Merthyr Mawr village in under a mile, passing Ton Farm once more.

At the village bear right at the green to the suspension footbridge. Over the bridge you have the same choice as the outward leg – ahead for the stepping stones, or left across the field and over the footbridge back to the road. Retrace your steps to the pub.

26 Llangynwyd
The Old House (Yr Hendy)

Dating back to 1147, this beautifully situated pub certainly lives up to its name. Probably one of the oldest licensed premises in Wales, it looks the part with a thatched roof, original beams and a large inglenook fireplace. The pub is one of the few places still to host the Welsh New Year tradition of Mari Lwyd, in which a decorated horse's head is taken from door to door. Incidentally an old photograph of the ceremony taking place in the village can be seen in the Folk Museum at St Fagans.

The interior is comfortable and roomy, with a conservatory restaurant area making the most of the panoramic views from its hilltop position. The same view is enjoyed by the large beer garden area with its excellent adventure playground. All food is freshly prepared and served in generous portions. The main menu has starters like grilled sardines and garlic prawns and the main courses include home-made steak and kidney pie, and trout with almonds. There are also specials, such as expertly cooked red snapper. Well-kept Brains SA and Flowers Original and IPA beers complete the picture.

Telephone: 0656 733310.

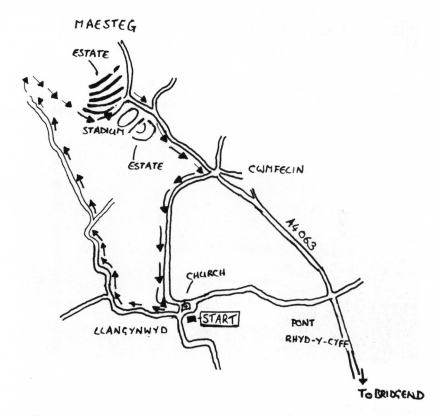

How to get there: Llangynwyd is on a minor road signposted 'Llan', from the A4063 south of Maesteg.

Parking: The pub has a large car park.

Length of the walk: About 3½ miles. Map: OS Landranger series 170 Vale of Glamorgan and Rhondda area (GR 857887).

A rewarding exploration, mainly on country lanes, of an attractive rural backwater, undisturbed by its closeness to a busy Valleys town.

The Walk

With your back to the pub, turn left and take the road to the left of another pub, the Corner House, descending past houses into an open lane. At a Y-junction turn right. Ignore a public footpath sign next to a gate, but take the open right turn, leading upwards on a narrow country lane between trees. The lane meanders along and, just before it dips sharply, pause to take in the view across the Llynfi valley to the mountains beyond.

Cross a small bridge and climb again towards a line of power pylons. At a junction turn left. The road soon peters out into a pleasant green lane straight ahead. Cross a stream and bear right at a junction of tracks towards an electricity pylon. As the track passes below the power lines, turn right on to a disused railway line passing in front of houses on the skyline.

You soon reach Maesteg Park Athletic Club ground. Turn left for a short section through a housing estate, turning right into Keir Hardie Road. Follow the road past the front of the clubhouse, carrying straight on to descend a hill – take care with children on the short section without pavement to the bottom of the hill.

Cross the bridge and turn right, signposted 'Llan'. This road climbs steadily back to Llangynwyd and the pub. Frequent pauses for breath can be justified on the grounds of enjoying the wildlife – I saw a pair of foxes crossing the road towards the top of the hill.

27 Kenfig
The Prince of Wales

Although the towers and chimneys of industrial Margam are visible on the skyline, it is a different world among the silent dunes and grasses of Kenfig Burrows. The Prince of Wales, one of a straggle of buildings which form Kenfig village, is on a minor road fronting a national nature reserve. Beneath the sands the ancient city of Cenfigg is said to be buried – castle and all.

Fresh food and fine beer are the hallmarks of this exemplary pub run by a landlord who grows much of the produce and has a big hand in the cooking. Fish, much of it caught off nearby Sker beach, is the inn's speciality, and the fisherman's platter is highly recommended. The choices on the board vary according to the catch – examples are fresh salmon or sewin, grilled or poached, and monkfish steak. Laverbread (seaweed), a Welsh delicacy, cooked with bacon or cockles is also collected locally. Other tempting options include pork ribs in spicy sauce and roast of the day. Real ales include Felinfoel Double Dragon, Bass, Marston's Pedigree, Worthington Best, Wadworth 6X plus guests like Adnams Broadside. Coal and log fires keep the stone-walled lounge and wood-panelled dining-room cosy in winter – and it's a place that is hard to leave at any time of year.

Telephone: 0656 740356.

FOOD - 12 TILL 2
7 TILL 10.

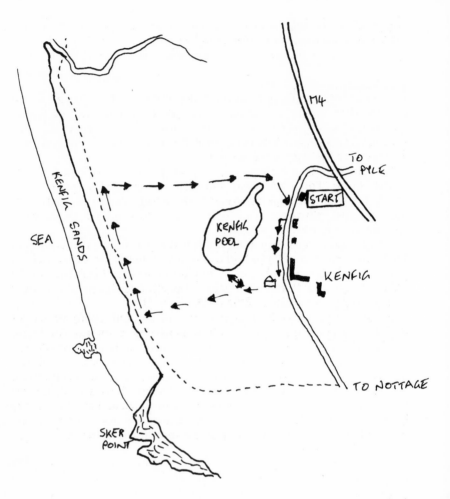

How to get there: The Prince of Wales is on a minor road and a little tricky to find, despite being close to the M4. The nearest motorway exit is junction 37, north of Porthcawl. Head through South Cornelly and just beyond the second roundabout after leaving the motorway, turn right. The pub is a couple of miles along this road.

Parking: The pub has a large car park and there is alternative parking at the nature reserve centre just 5 minutes' walk away.

Length of the walk: About 3 miles. Map: OS Landranger series 170 Vale of Glamorgan and Rhondda area (GR 804818).

A wonderful exploration of an unusual nature reserve, weaving through its extra-ordinary dune landscape, with a short stretch by the sea and a visit to a large pool — the largest natural freshwater pool in Glamorgan — famous among bird-watchers.

The Walk

With your back to the pub, turn left down the road, crossing over to use a roadside path. After about 5 minutes, turn right into the nature reserve. It's worth popping into the visitor centre – we arrived just as an injured buzzard was being brought in and had the rare chance for an eyeball-to-eyeball close look.

Take the path leading from the car park into the reserve to the right of the centre. This path twists and turns for about 1½ miles to the beach. It's well worth taking a right-hand detour about 150 yards from the car park, however, to reach Kenfig Pool and a large, well-appointed hide for bird-watchers.

Retrace your steps to where you left the main path and continue. There are a number of paths and tracks lacing the sandy, grass-covered terrain and it is easy to stray – but don't worry. Keep the smoke stacks of industrial Port Talbot (incredibly close to this peaceful place) to your right and you will eventually reach the sea.

The beach lies beyond a final barrier of dunes. Our route turns right to follow a good track just inside that barrier. Continue for about 10 minutes (about ½ mile) until you reach a large bowl-shaped depression to the right. The path you want is pretty clear, climbing a dune on the far edge of the depression, but to make sure keep an eye out for an upright sawn-off tree trunk beside the track. Strike off inland at 90° from the seaside track. Stick to the main path all the way back. It trends rightwards past the fringes of the pool to emerge on the road at a bus stop almost opposite the Prince of Wales.

28 Tonna
The Whittington Arms

Despite the pub sign featuring the familiar panto character, the pub has little connection with spotted hankies, cats or turning again. In fact the hillside inn was once the home of a Dr Whittington who practised early this century in the quiet Vale of Neath village. Sitting in the waiting room and taking your medicine is much more fun these days!

The Whit, as it is known, is a friendly local, unexpectedly large and roomy, with a good selection of wholesome food. Most popular are standards such as steak and kidney pie, lasagne and curries. There is a children's menu, too, offering favourites like burgers and chicken nuggets. Sunday is traditional roast time and a standard meal – home-made soup, a choice from three meats with fresh vegetables, followed by a sweet – is served, with smaller portions of the same for children. Regular real ales include Worthington Best and Bass, and they are supplemented by a guest ale, for example, Winter Royal. Benches in the walled-off car park at the front are a popular summer option – the road is not terribly busy. Overnight accommodation is also available, if you want a longer stay.

Telephone: 0639 643229.

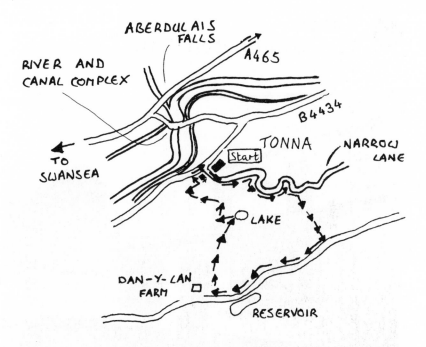

How to get there: The pub is on the B4434 next to the church in Tonna, less than 2 miles north-east of Neath.

Parking: The pub has ample parking space.

Length of the walk: 2½ miles. Map: OS Landranger series 170 Vale of Glamorgan and Rhondda area (GR 775990).

A walk full of interest, which is kept quite short to allow time to visit the Aberdulais Falls, within easy walking distance below the pub. The walk climbs high above the village, giving excellent views to the Brecon Beacons and across the vale to Swansea Bay.

The Walk

Leave the pub at the front and turn left and immediately left again up a lane rising between a church hall and the pub wall. Keep climbing straight ahead as the lane becomes a narrow path, ignoring steps to the right.

You soon emerge on a road opposite houses with a three-way bridleway signpost. Turn left and continue on the main lane, ignoring small turnings and drives. It swings sharp right, then left. Shortly after passing two houses below and to the left, and crossing high above a stream, keep an eye out for a stile with a tall public footpath signpost on the right. Cross over into a soggy area, criss-crossed with streams and churned up by ponies. Go straight ahead for a few yards to reach a rough track, then bear left for 30 yards or so to negotiate a six-bar metal gate with the platform of a stile before it.

Go straight ahead on an obvious path through the trees. At a vague fork bear right, passing a bricked-up mine tunnel to your left. The path becomes more defined and there is a small zigzag before reaching some rough open ground. Aim for a white house on the skyline above you. You will soon see a stile to the right of the house.

Cross the stile on to a minor road and turn right. Enjoy the easy downward stroll and superb views across to the right and back up the valley. Closer at hand, in fields below and to the right, are the ruins of the Ivy Tower, an 18th century folly which you will pass close to later.

Carry on down the lane, passing farms and houses, and it soon becomes quite narrow between walls. Pass a reservoir below to the left with attractive cascades. Shortly after passing the reservoir gates, reach the signposted entrance to Dan-y-lan Farm. Go through a signposted gate to the right of the entrance and follow the diagonal path, climbing rightwards towards another signpost. The Ivy Tower is above to the right, but access appears to be prohibited. The track passes behind the farm buildings to a clearing. Ahead and to the left of the clearing a good path descends into woodland beside a tumble-down wall. Go through a gate and continue to a T-junction with another track.

A small detour here to the 'echoing lake', a quarry pool, is worth while. A couple of yards before the junction, turn right into the brush and after a few yards you will reach the pool edge, completely hidden from the path. Try shouting – it does echo.

Return to the junction, turn left and, after 50 yards, turn right onto a descending path. The track soon passes gardens and brings you to a residential street, Mount Pleasant. Turn left and at Tonna memorial gates, turn right and bear right along Dolcoed Terrace. At a crossroads, turn left and descend to the B4434. Turn right to return to the pub.

Oldwalls
The Greyhound Inn

(29)

Originally a farmhouse, when the Greyhound became a pub it catered for farmers driving cattle on foot to market. Nowadays customers on foot are usually out for a day's exercise, though there are still plenty of farmers among the regulars. It retains the atmosphere of a local, tucked away in a straggle of homes on the quieter north side of the Gower peninsula.

Locally caught seafood along with meat and game from nearby farms and shoots are specialities here and the menu features local produce. The ploughman's lunch with a selection of Welsh cheeses, cawl (a hearty Welsh soup) or Welsh lamb marinated in wine and herbs are among the options. There are also curries and chillies, which may not be traditionally Welsh but they are certainly made on the premises. Fish, such as pollack or fresh cod fillet, and game appear according to availability. Meals do not cost an arm and a leg and this is one of the few pubs which offers meals for two – Sunday lunch, for example, could be a roast joint of beef surrounded by vegetables on a large platter complete with carving knife. There is a good, reasonably priced children's menu, too. Boddingtons and Bass are the regular real ales, joined by two or three guests like Flowers IPA and Wadworth 6X. The pub has a beer garden to the rear and a games room attached to the bar.

Telephone: 0792 390146.

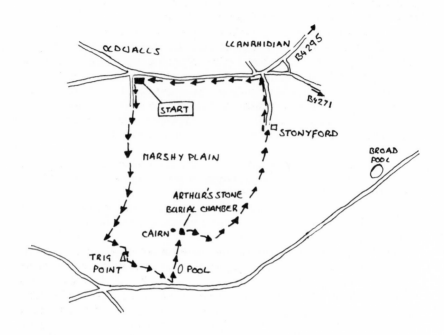

How to get there: The hamlet of Oldwalls is just west of Llanrhidian and the junction of the B4271 and the B4295 on the north coast of the Gower Peninsula.

Parking: There is a large car park beside the pub.

Length of the walk: About 4½ miles. Map: OS Landranger series 159 Swansea, Gower and surrounding area, or OS Pathfinder series 1126 Gower (GR 487919).

A nice change from lounging on the beach – an upland excursion which shows the other side of Gower. It also offers outstanding views and a chance to visit Arthur's Stone, a place of magic for centuries. King Arthur's ghost, clad in gleaming armour, is said to appear from time to time.

The Walk

With your back to the pub, turn left and, immediately past the pub, turn left again down a lane marked with a footpath post. Walk straight on through a gate and up a rough track to another gate. Beyond the gate you emerge on open moorland – it is pretty marshy for a while and it pays to choose your footing with care.

Go straight ahead on a well-trodden track which you can see marching up the hillside ahead of you. As you pass under a line of cables, keep to the right-hand path, climbing the slope. The track levels out, trending slightly rightwards across a small grassy plateau. To your left you should be able to see a trig point – if you cannot because of mist I would recommend calling the walk off and retracing your steps for an early lunch. The area is laced with paths and while the basic route is straightforward it would be easy to stray in poor visibility.

Assuming you can see clearly, look back for a wide seascape beyond the pub. Carry on to reach a junction of several grassy paths and take the left-hand path, more or less at 90° to the one you arrived on, ignoring the nearest path on your left which turns almost back on yourself. In other words, treat it as a roundabout and take the second left.

Carry on down this broad, springy path for about 60 yards and then take a path to the right leading upwards to the trig point. At the pillar turn left along the top of the hill on a broad track, which quickly leads to a popular parking area beside a minor road. At the grassy layby, turn left along a very broad path, passing a tarn to your right. The track swings to the right and soon approaches a massive boulder, actually the capstone of an ancient burial chamber known as Arthur's Stone. In legend, King Arthur is supposed to have thrown the stone from a spot 7 miles away when he was troubled by the 'pebble' in his shoe – a good trick. A large cairn to the left is also worth visiting.

Continue rightwards from Arthur's Stone on the good track. If followed all the way this track would go full circle back to the car park. About 250 yards from the stone, keep a close eye out for a vague path descending to the left into the valley you crossed earlier on the outward leg. You should be able to see the line of the path going over the valley plain below you to a barn.

The path soon becomes much clearer, though soggy. Keep heading for the barn, well to the right of a white farmhouse. Just to the left of the tin barn and a house – Stonyford on the map – cross a stile and go straight ahead up a surfaced lane.

You soon emerge on the B4271 beside the North Gower Hotel where you turn left and then left again at a junction to return to the Greyhound. Take care on this section of road as there is no pavement for much of it.

30 **Rhossili**
The Worm's Head Hotel

Set in a designated area of outstanding natural beauty, much of it owned by the National Trust, the views from this coastal hotel are sensational. To one side the huge sweep of sandy Rhossili Bay, to the other the headland which gives the place its name juts out to sea. You may be lucky enough to see seals and dolphins here. Rhossili, at the western tip of the Gower Peninsula, is a small village literally at the end of the line. Nevertheless, the place is a magnet for surfers, wind surfers and hang gliders. The 3 miles of sands backed by grassy upland are tailor-made for lovers of outdoor activity.

Picnic tables placed outside the hotel in summer make the most of the hotel's position and the view from the restaurant is panoramic. The emphasis of the menu is on home cooking, with plenty of fresh fish. On the board you may find such items as ham, lentil and vegetable soup, grilled trout with almonds and home-made corned beef pasty and chips. The lunch menu in the Ocean Room restaurant features main courses like fresh salmon, plaice or sole, minted lamb chops and duck à l'orange. Worthington Best is the real ale on offer, along with Guinness and the usual range of lagers and ciders. The hotel has 20 bedrooms, all with a sea view.

Telephone: 0792 390512.

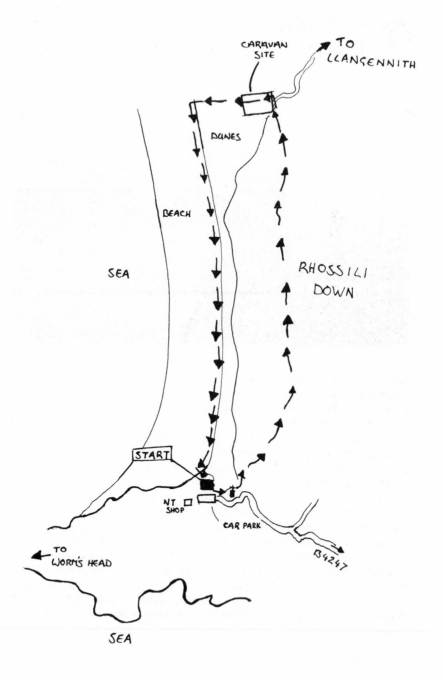

TO LLANGENNITH

CARAVAN SITE

DUNES

BEACH

SEA

RHOSSILI DOWN

START

NT SHOP

CAR PARK

TO WORM'S HEAD

SEA

B4247

How to get there: The hotel is adjacent to the car park in Rhossili, at the end of the B4247 at the south-western tip of the Gower Peninsula.

Parking: The hotel car park is small and hard to find. It may be better to use the large public car park alongside, for which a modest daily charge is made in summer.

Length of the walk: A little over 4 miles. Map: OS Landranger series 159 Swansea, Gower and surrounding area (GR 415881).

A lovely circuit which heads out along National Trust-owned Rhossili Down with fine views and returns along the magnificent beach. On a hot day the return leg might take some time! Route-finding is easy and the walk presents no difficulties, though there are some steep climbs and descents.

The Walk

With your back to the hotel front, turn left inland along the road towards the church. Just before the churchyard, turn left along a narrow path which runs around the back of it. When you have rounded the churchyard, turn left down a lane and through a wooden gate by a National Trust notice. Bear right steeply uphill (signposted 'Hill End'), initially by reinforced steps. Take it steadily and the path levels slightly before climbing again to the top of Rhossili Down. Swing left past a trig point beacon on the very broad, good track and head almost due north. Navigation is easy – just keep the sea to your left and stay on the main track, enjoying the magnificent views and sea breezes.

Eventually you pass just to the right of a rocky outcrop. Keep to the high ground, bearing slightly left and the path starts descending, leaving a spur off to the right. The caravans of the Hillend site soon come into view – follow the steep path to the entrance at the far right corner.

Turn left into the site and follow the road straight ahead to a parking area in front of the dunes. At the car park take an exit on the right, which leads through the dunes to the beach. Turn left here, and walk back all the way along the beach. As you near the southern end of the bay, take the concrete steps climbing to the left. The path swings right and emerges beside the hotel.